OFFICERS & SOLDI

ARTILLERY
1786-1815
THE GRIBEAUVAL SYSTEM

Volume III. The Pontoneers, the Bridge Teams, Siege Artillery, Stronghold and Coastal Artillery, Coastal Gunners, Permanent Gunners, Veterans, the Team Trains and Regimental Artillery

Ludovic LETRUN
and Jean-Marie MONGIN

Translated from the French by Alan McKAY

Histoire & Collections

THE PONTONEERS

Ever since the 18th century, the Pontoneers' job was to find ways of crossing rivers: boat bridges, mobile bridges or improvised trestles bridges. Boat bridges were either made with little boats rooted out on the spot or with pontoons (flat-bottomed square-ended boats) that the army brought up from the rear. The copper pontoons imagined by Colonel Martinet in 1672, copying the Dutch were kept until 12 Floréal An-XI (2 May 1803) when a decree replaced them by so-called *"avant-garde"* boats.

The mobile bridges were "ferries" guided across the river along a cable attached to both banks.

Building bridges meant transporting a lot of equipment and this was why the Pontoneers, in the French Army, were part of the Artillery rather than the Engineers. It was an unending subject for discussion between the two learned arms.

The creation of the Pontoneers

The Pontoneers of the time were created in 1792 when two companies of *Bateliers du Rhin* (Rhine boatmen) were formed at Strasburg and were at the origins of the *Matelots du Rhin* (the Rhine Sailors) in 1793. A law dated 18 Floréal An III (7 May 1795) assigned this battalion, which in the meantime had become the *"Pontoneers Corps"*, to the Artillery.

The corps' job was to build and look after the bridges over the Rhine. It comprised a headquarters and eight companies, making a total of 597 men. A Second Battalion, set up in the same way, was created for the Army of the Sambre and the Meuse in 1795.

BATTALION HEADQUARTERS AND THE PONTONEER COMPANY

The Headquarters
1 battalion commander
1 quartermaster treasurer
1 adjudant
1 master tailor
1 master cobbler

The company
1 captain commanding
1 sergeant-major
2 sergeants
1 corporal-furrier
4 corporals
1 drummer
7 workers
56 pontoneers

"In France, they (the Pontoneers) are part of the Artillery even though the two sorts of manoeuvres have nothing in common; but the Artillery's extensive means of transport and the precautions it takes for the security of its pools mean it is easier for it to move the pontoneers, their equipment and their gear." (Bardin, Dictionnaire)

The following year the provisional companies were created for the Army of Italy using the Lombard boatmen. It was only on 23 Fructidor An VII (9 September 1799) that the number of battalions was fixed at two.

The corps comprised 1,198 pontoneers including officers and a battalion was made up of 599 soldiers in eight companies. On 27 December 1800 General Marmont organised a short-lived Third Battalion with the provisional companies from the Army of Italy and the companies from the defunct Army of the Sambre and Meuse.

On 10 October 1801, these pontoneers were sent to the Second Battalion, attached to the Army of Italy. The First Battalion was assigned to the operations on the Rhine, the second was used on the other side of the Alps.

During the Empire

With the Empire's increasing number of fronts, the battalions were reorganised as and when the needs of the campaigns changed. On 13 July 1808, the 2nd and 3rd Companies of the Second Battalion went over to the 1st which then had ten companies. Four companies from the First Battalion and one from the 2nd left for the Iberian Peninsula.

The battalions were reorganised on 16 March 1809, to reform the units and also create a depot at Strasburg: the 1st had 10 companies, the 2nd six. The depot was commanded by a second captain.

On 10 October 1810, the First Battalion absorbed the Pontoneer Company from the Kingdom of Holland, increasing to 11 companies. In 1812, seven companies from the First Battalion were assigned to the *Grande Armée* and left for Russia. The Second Battalion was assigned to the Army of the Viceroy of Italy, Eugène de Beauharnais.

THE PONTONEERS

Drummer in the Strasbourg Pontoneers wearing a revised *à la Henri IV* hat with a tricolour plume. The national blue coat is decorated with tricolour braid on the lapels, the facings, the collar and the turnback. The grey-blue drum surrounded with the tricolour bears a green laurel wreath with a golden anchor, a P (for Pontoneers) above and R (Rhine) underneath. *(after Tanconville).*

Pontoneer NCO wearing town dress in about 1793-1804.

Pontoneers from 1793 onwards, wearing a uniform close to that of the Light Artillery. The pontoneers' coat was cut from national blue cloth, edged with scarlet on the pointed lapels, the shoulder flaps and the collar. The pointed facings, the lining, the waistcoat, the breech knots and the tassels of the half-gaiters were scarlet. The copper uniform button was stamped with an anchor.

From 1793 to 1803, the Pontoneer Corps only used a tricolour pennant with vertical stripes, with the blue closest to the shaft, surmounted by a white metal pike. On both sides, in the middle, was a laurel wreath with a golden anchor in its centre, with the letter P above and the letter R beneath it.

CROSSING THE BEREZINA

The pontoneers' devotion to duty during the crossing of the Berezina is well known. *"Urged on and supported by the presence of General Eblé, the pontoneers showed limitless perseverance and dedication while repairing the bridges; out of more than 100 who went into the water either to built or to repair the bridges, only a small number survived.*

[...] *Among all those martyrs to duty, one name alone remains known to history, that of General Eblé who died a month later; but his name covers in glory those of the 400 unsung heroes, the survivors of 2,000, who were equal in their hearts to their venerable commander."*

(Historique du Corps des Pontonniers)

The First Battalion, under the command of General Eblé, with a strength of 400 pontoneers, worked in merciless conditions to build bridges over the Berezina at the Studianka ford and disappeared during the retreat. At Mainz, a decree dated 18 April 1813 replaced the seven defunct companies from the First Battalion with six new companies made up of men from the depot and sailors from the 17th Flotilla Crew. A six-company Third Battalion was created on the same day. The Saxon Campaign was awful for the Pontoneers and all the companies were decimated or taken prisoner. In October, the surviving pontoneers, sailors and workers from the fleet were assembled and, on 18 November, the First Battalion – theoretically made up of 14 companies – was reformed.

Thirteen days later on 1 December, the Second Battalion was increased to 8 companies. The Pontoneers Company of the Imperial Guard was set up in April 1814 and the 12 May 1814 Ordnance brought together the 3 battalions' scattered pontoneers into one battalion with eight companies (11th, 12th, 13th, 14th, two in Italy at Turin – the 7th and 8th – together with those recovered from the Army of Spain).

In May 1815, during the Hundred Days, the battalion was increased to ten companies. The first five and the 8th were with the Army of the North and served in Belgium. After Waterloo, the Pontoneer Battalion in the new Royal Army was made up from the 6th and the 7th Companies. The companies from the Army of the North were disbanded at Limoges in November 1815.

THE SIEGE ARTILLERY

The *Grande Armée* carried out sieges all during the Empire; in this case the gunners served specific pieces, mainly howitzers.

A howitzer fired along a curved trajectory which could go over defensive walls. The 8-in howitzer cannonballs (almost 46 lbs without the powder charge) were heavy and deadly but the gunners were not satisfied with the calibres. One mustn't forget that all this firing used up a lot of powder and made the guns fragile, reducing their life span which was already short. In the initial pages of the novel by Arturo Perez Reverte, *Cadix ou la diagonale du fou*, all the difficulties that the French gunners ran into during a siege are described very vividly. It was during this particular siege that the Armaments Commission decided to cast bigger calibre guns – 24-inch or even 36-inch. The besiegers also put into operation another gun: the mortar, in particular the 10-in mortar. The mortar weighed more than 1,719 lbs and propelled its explosive 110-lb "bomb" over distances ranging from 1,750 yd to 2,406 yd. These bombs were fired over the walls or were used to destroy them, or to carry out saturation bombing against the enemy batteries. The French siege artillery was formidably effective and its calibres fairly homogenous, enabling cities such as Danzig, Valencia, Saragossa and Tarragon to be captured.

STRONGHOLD ARTILLERY

Stronghold Artillery – and this hadn't varied ever since Vauban – used the same mortars as those used by the besiegers. The mortar had to be able to fire over the walls, in one direction or the other. The cannon set up in batteries on the ramparts were somewhat different from those used by campaign artillery. Indeed, rather than firing through the loopholes in the walls – not a very practical proposition for azimuth shooting – the guns were mounted on raised carriages enabling them to fire over the parapet. The disadvantage for the defenders was that these guns were very vulnerable to the attackers' counter-batteries. Here again the permanent companies or the veterans' companies served the stronghold guns.

(Continued on page 20)

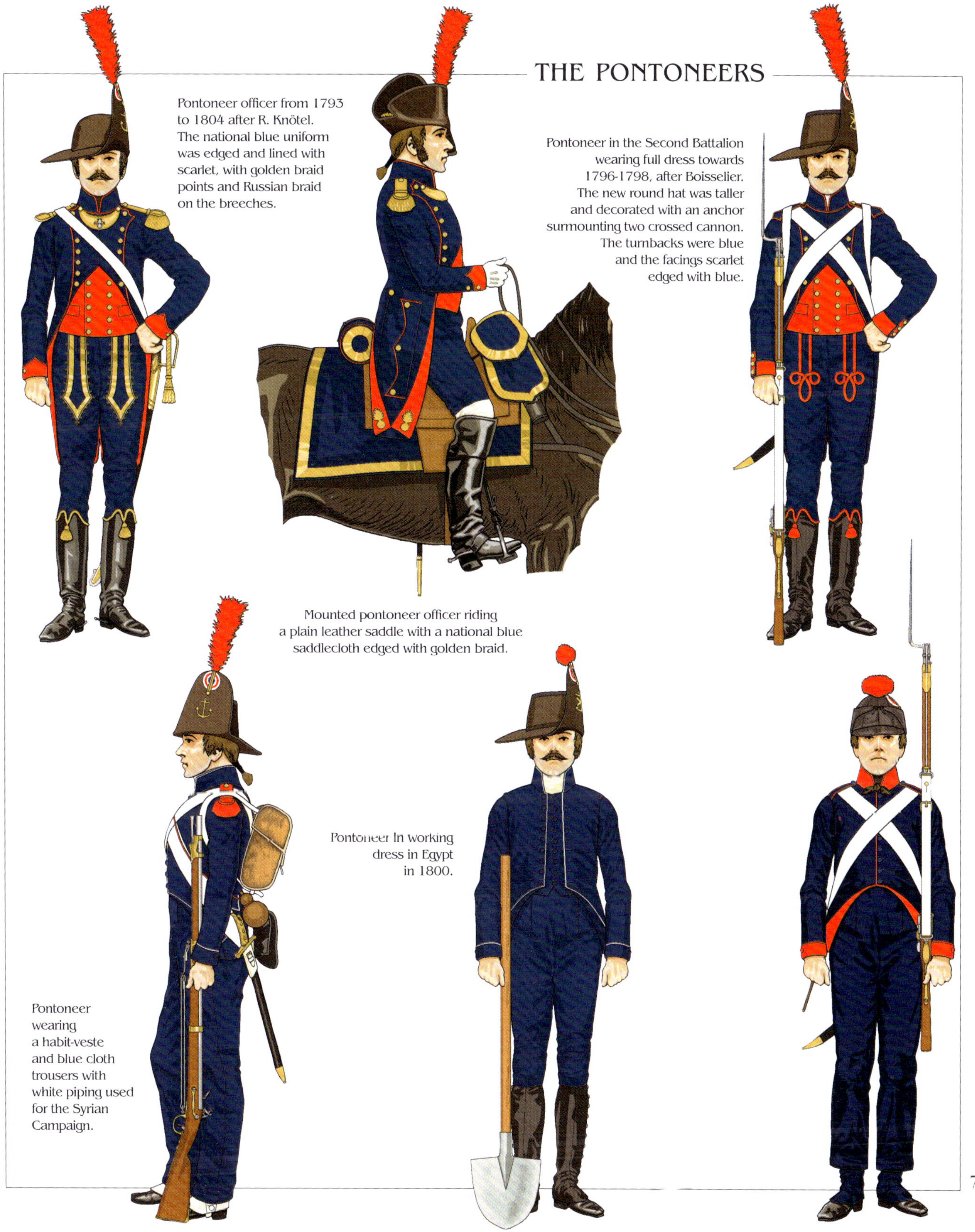

Pontoneer officer from 1793 to 1804 after R. Knötel. The national blue uniform was edged and lined with scarlet, with golden braid points and Russian braid on the breeches.

Pontoneer in the Second Battalion wearing full dress towards 1796-1798, after Boisselier. The new round hat was taller and decorated with an anchor surmounting two crossed cannon. The turnbacks were blue and the facings scarlet edged with blue.

Mounted pontoneer officer riding a plain leather saddle with a national blue saddlecloth edged with golden braid.

Pontoneer in working dress in Egypt in 1800.

Pontoneer wearing a habit-veste and blue cloth trousers with white piping used for the Syrian Campaign.

THE PONTONEERS

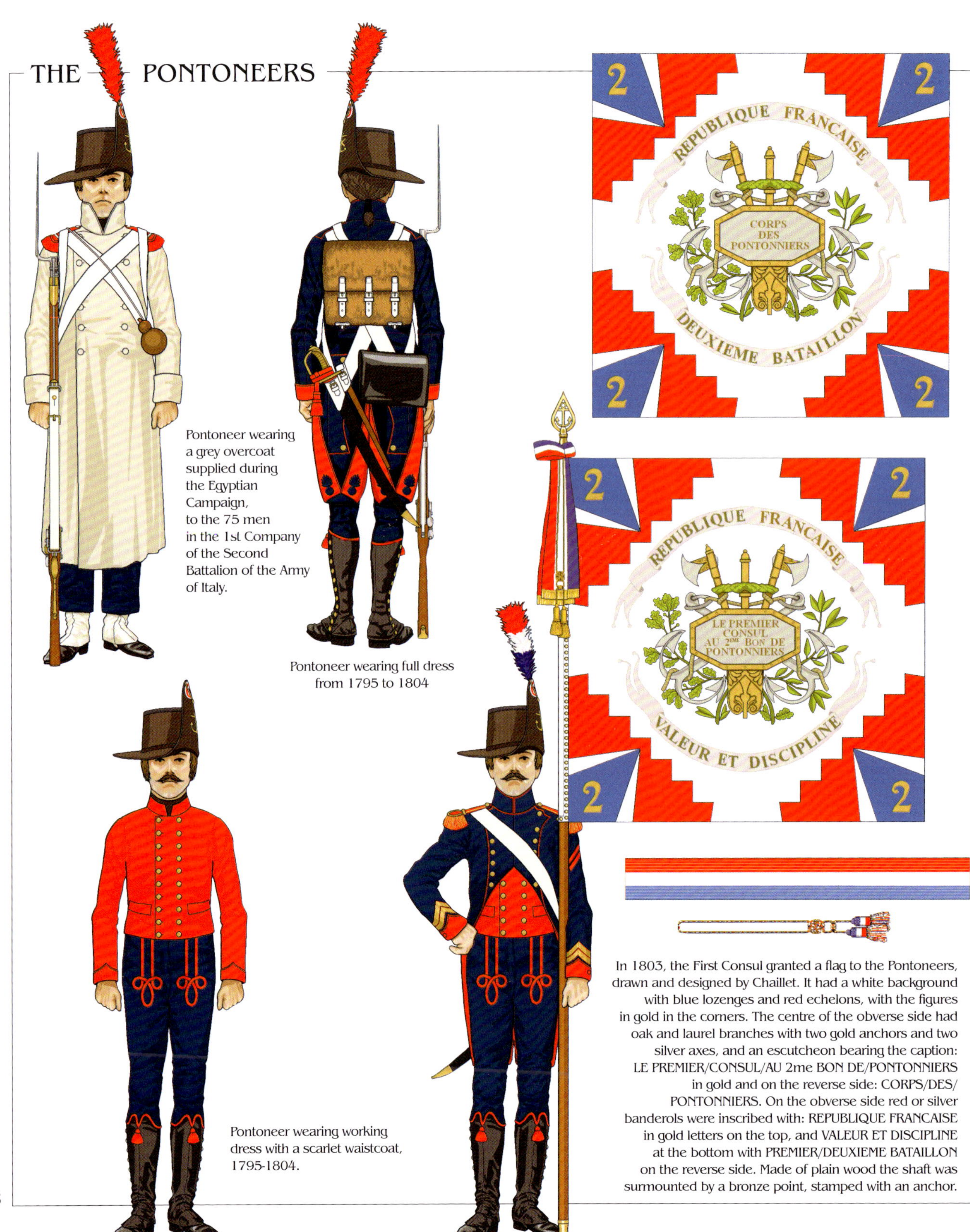

Pontoneer wearing a grey overcoat supplied during the Egyptian Campaign, to the 75 men in the 1st Company of the Second Battalion of the Army of Italy.

Pontoneer wearing full dress from 1795 to 1804

Pontoneer wearing working dress with a scarlet waistcoat, 1795-1804.

In 1803, the First Consul granted a flag to the Pontoneers, drawn and designed by Chaillet. It had a white background with blue lozenges and red echelons, with the figures in gold in the corners. The centre of the obverse side had oak and laurel branches with two gold anchors and two silver axes, and an escutcheon bearing the caption: LE PREMIER/CONSUL/AU 2me BON DE/PONTONNIERS in gold and on the reverse side: CORPS/DES/ PONTONNIERS. On the obverse side red or silver banderols were inscribed with: REPUBLIQUE FRANCAISE in gold letters on the top, and VALEUR ET DISCIPLINE at the bottom with PREMIER/DEUXIEME BATAILLON on the reverse side. Made of plain wood the shaft was surmounted by a bronze point, stamped with an anchor.

THE PONTONEERS

Officer from a pontoneer company, equipped with a tinplate megaphone towards 1804-1812. From 1804 onwards, the Pontoneer Corps adopted the dark blue uniform of the Foot Artillery.

Pontoneer wearing Guard's uniform in about 1806-1812.

On 5 December 1804, the two-pontoneer battalions each received an eagle and a Picot-style flag. The inscriptions on the cloth are unknown to us but would most likely have been, on the obverse side: L'EMPEREUR/DES FRANCAIS/ AU… BATAILLON/DE PONTONNIERS, and VALEUR /ET/ DISCIPLINE on the reverse side.

The shako decorated with a lozenge-shaped plate with the number of the battalion, replaced the round hat from 1805-1806 onwards.

Pontoneer drummer in about 1806-1812, after Rousselot.

Pontoneer Battalion Commander wearing town dress at the beginning of the Empire

THE PONTONEERS

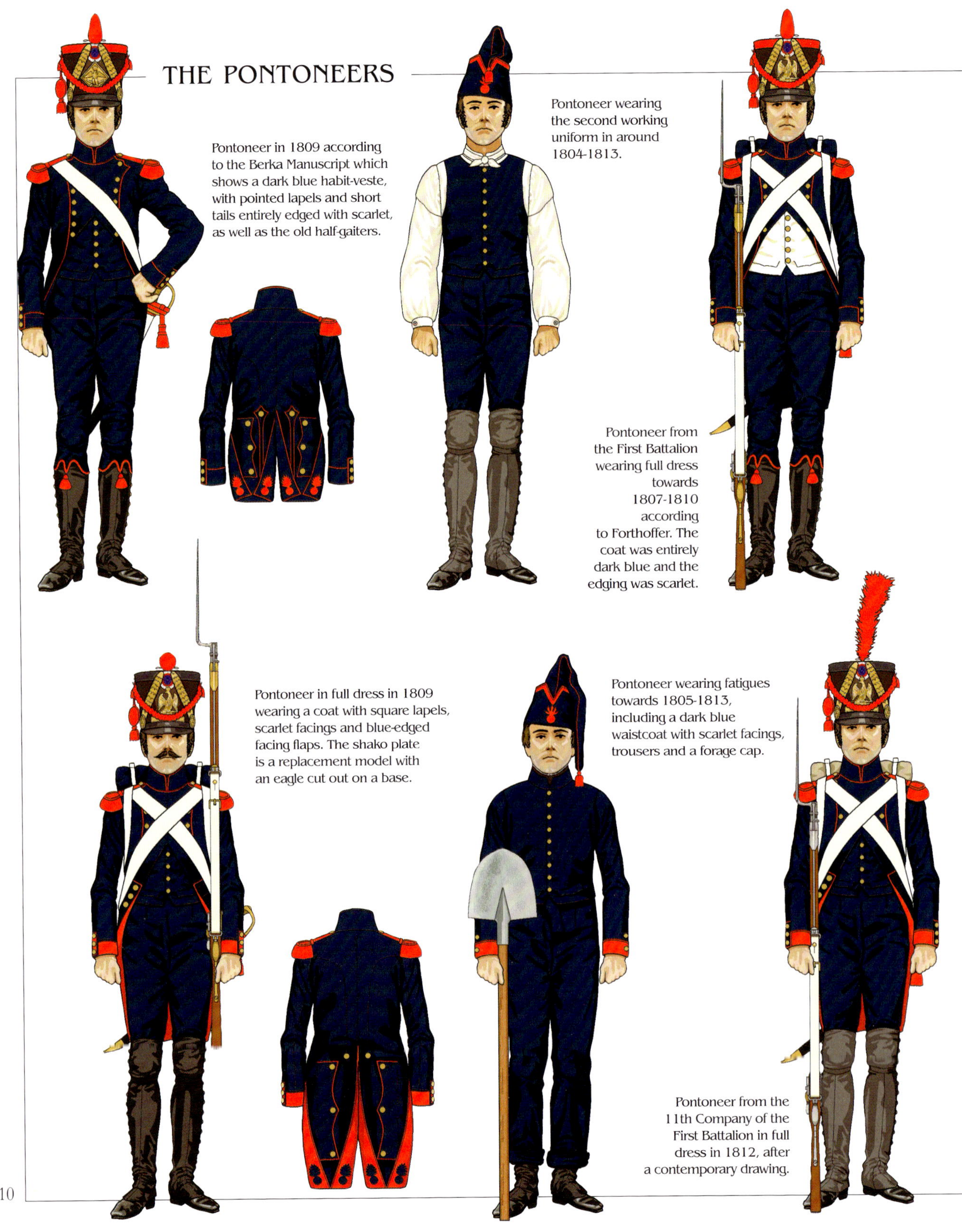

Pontoneer in 1809 according to the Berka Manuscript which shows a dark blue habit-veste, with pointed lapels and short tails entirely edged with scarlet, as well as the old half-gaiters.

Pontoneer wearing the second working uniform in around 1804-1813.

Pontoneer from the First Battalion wearing full dress towards 1807-1810 according to Forthoffer. The coat was entirely dark blue and the edging was scarlet.

Pontoneer in full dress in 1809 wearing a coat with square lapels, scarlet facings and blue-edged facing flaps. The shako plate is a replacement model with an eagle cut out on a base.

Pontoneer wearing fatigues towards 1805-1813, including a dark blue waistcoat with scarlet facings, trousers and a forage cap.

Pontoneer from the 11th Company of the First Battalion in full dress in 1812, after a contemporary drawing.

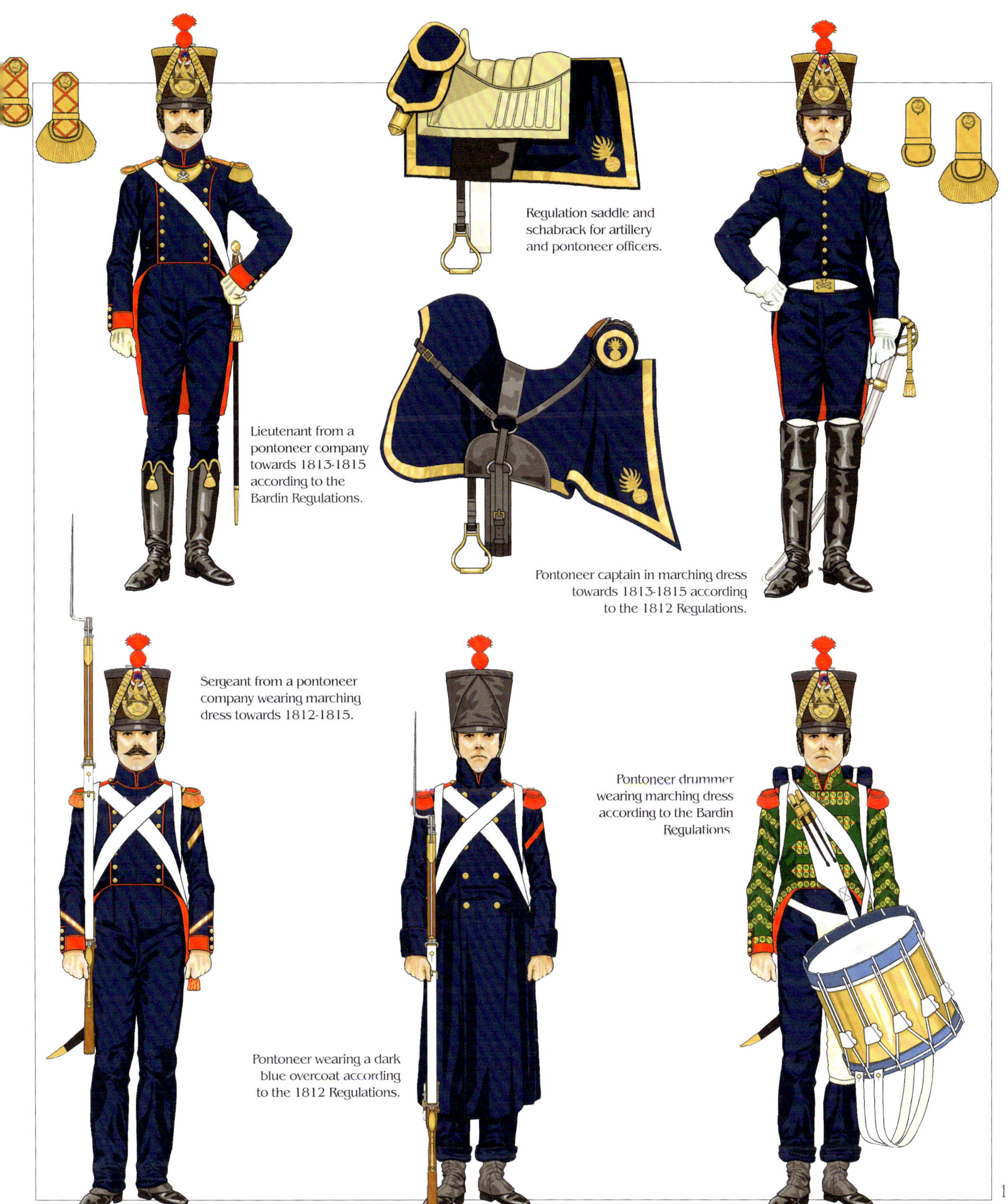

Regulation saddle and schabrack for artillery and pontoneer officers.

Lieutenant from a pontoneer company towards 1813-1815 according to the Bardin Regulations.

Pontoneer captain in marching dress towards 1813-1815 according to the 1812 Regulations.

Sergeant from a pontoneer company wearing marching dress towards 1812-1815.

Pontoneer drummer wearing marching dress according to the Bardin Regulations.

Pontoneer wearing a dark blue overcoat according to the 1812 Regulations.

1812- model artillery shako plate in use in the Pontoneer Corps.

Pontoneer uniform button made of copper stamped with the battalion number.

Pontoneer corporal wearing guard's dress according to the 1812 Regulations.

In 1812 the old eagles were sent back to the Ministry of War to be replaced by the single 1812-model eagle and the cloth had an inscription on the obverse side: L'EMPEREUR/NAPOLEON/ AUX BATAILLONS/ DE PONTONNEIRS. What was inscribed on the reverse side is not known.

In 1815, a new eagle with flag, tassels and cravat, was granted to the Pontoneer Corps and kept in Paris; the cloth of the 1815-model flag would probably have borne the same inscriptions as the 1812 one.

Pontoneer in working dress with a blue collar on a white waistcoat, according to the 1812 Regulations

Pontoneer wearing full dress according to the 1812 Regulations.

THE GRIBEAUVAL FORGE

This model was put into service by Gribeauval in 1769 and was still in use during the Empire in strongholds, coastal batteries or siege batteries. A new model with four wheels was brought in during An XI (see Volume 1).

This older model of forge was intended for flat terrain and was drawn by three horses; it comprised a cart with shafts, a furnace hearth, a bellows, an anvil and a tool coffer holding the blacksmith's hammer, tongs, spade and bucket.

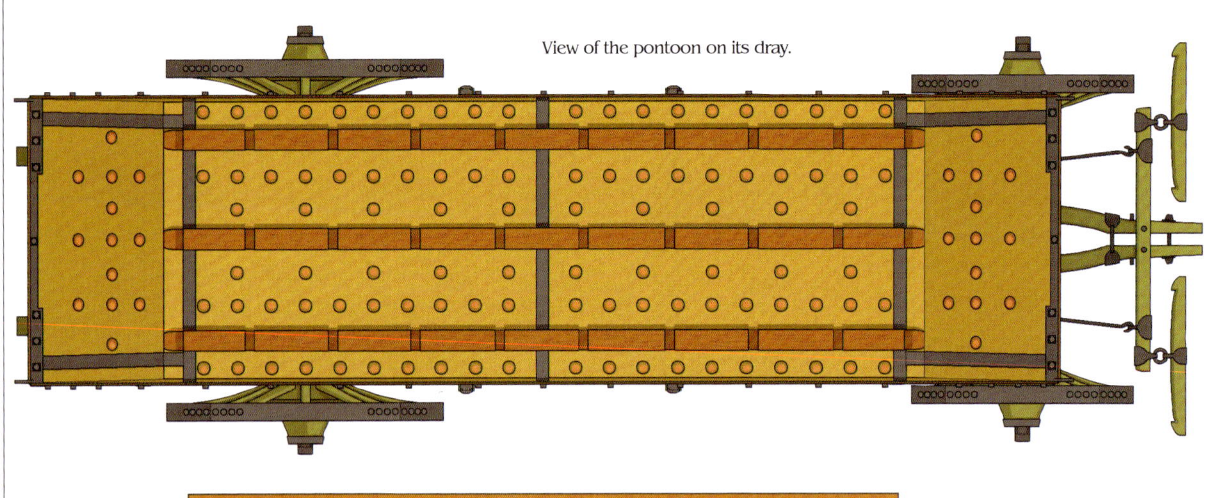

View of the pontoon on its dray.

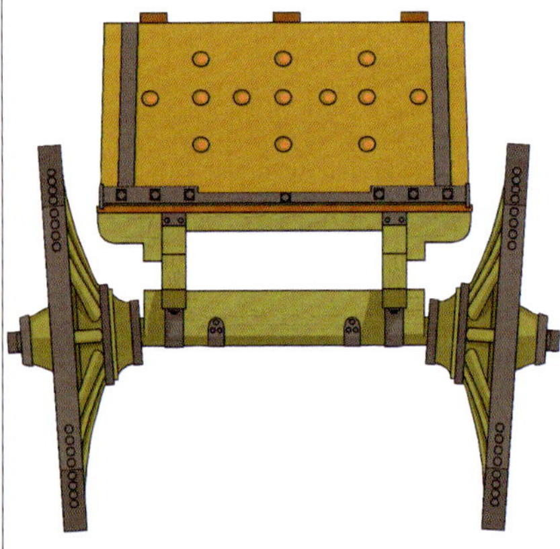

The advantage of the complete Gribeauval system of 36 copper pontoons was that it was lighter than the boat bridge and it could be moved around to follow the army more easily. The pontoon was 19 ft 1 ½ in long, 5 ft 3 in wide and 2 ft 6 in high. The elm framework was entirely covered with 540 lb of copper sheeting fixed by 176 lb of solder and nails.

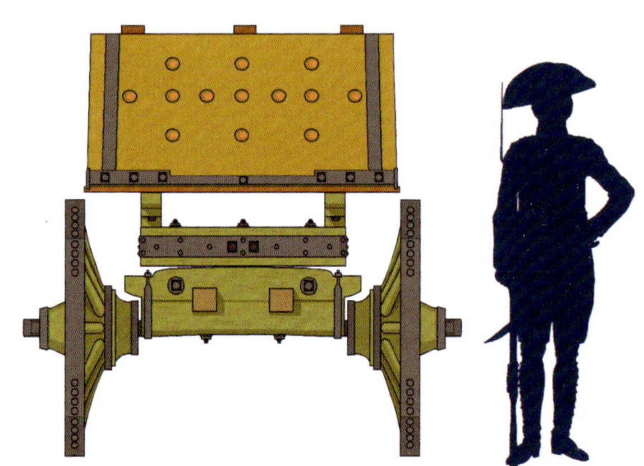

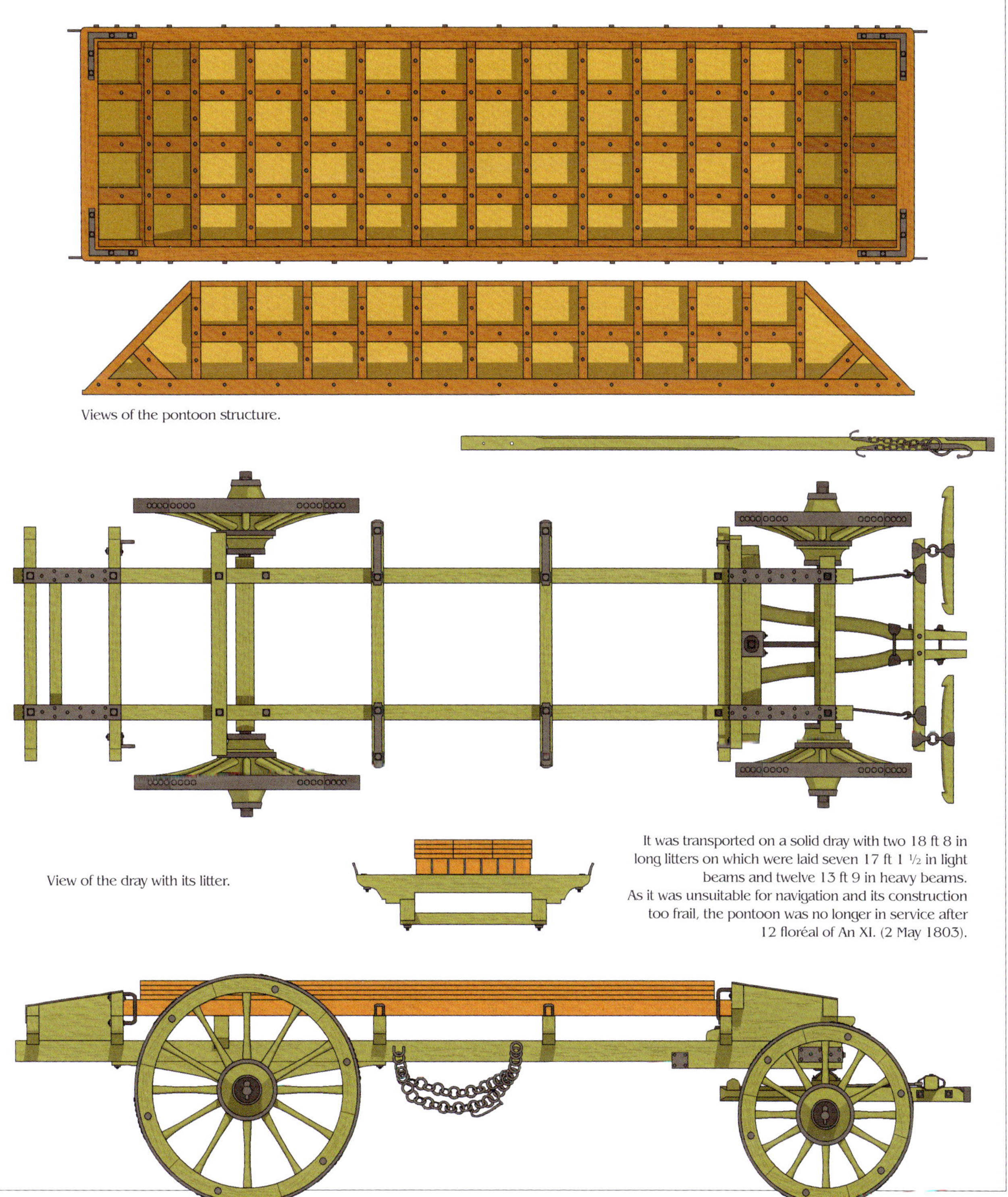

Views of the pontoon structure.

View of the dray with its litter.

It was transported on a solid dray with two 18 ft 8 in long litters on which were laid seven 17 ft 1 ½ in light beams and twelve 13 ft 9 in heavy beams. As it was unsuitable for navigation and its construction too frail, the pontoon was no longer in service after 12 floréal of An XI. (2 May 1803).

THE GRIBEAUVAL SYSTEM ARTILLERY TEAM BOAT

The model of artillery boat-bridge, perfected by Gribeauval, was still in service in the armies of the Republic with certain contingent changes. In theory each river had its boat bridge whose particular dimensions had been established in the arsenals in advance. As far as was possible, the boats were brought up by river, or failing that, by road on drays drawn by eight horses. The Gribeauval model was 36 ft 8 in long, 7 ft 3 in wide, 3 ft 11 in high and weighed 4,189 lbs. It was placed on a dray with a wagon pole, the heavy beams and the small beams being carried in another wagon.

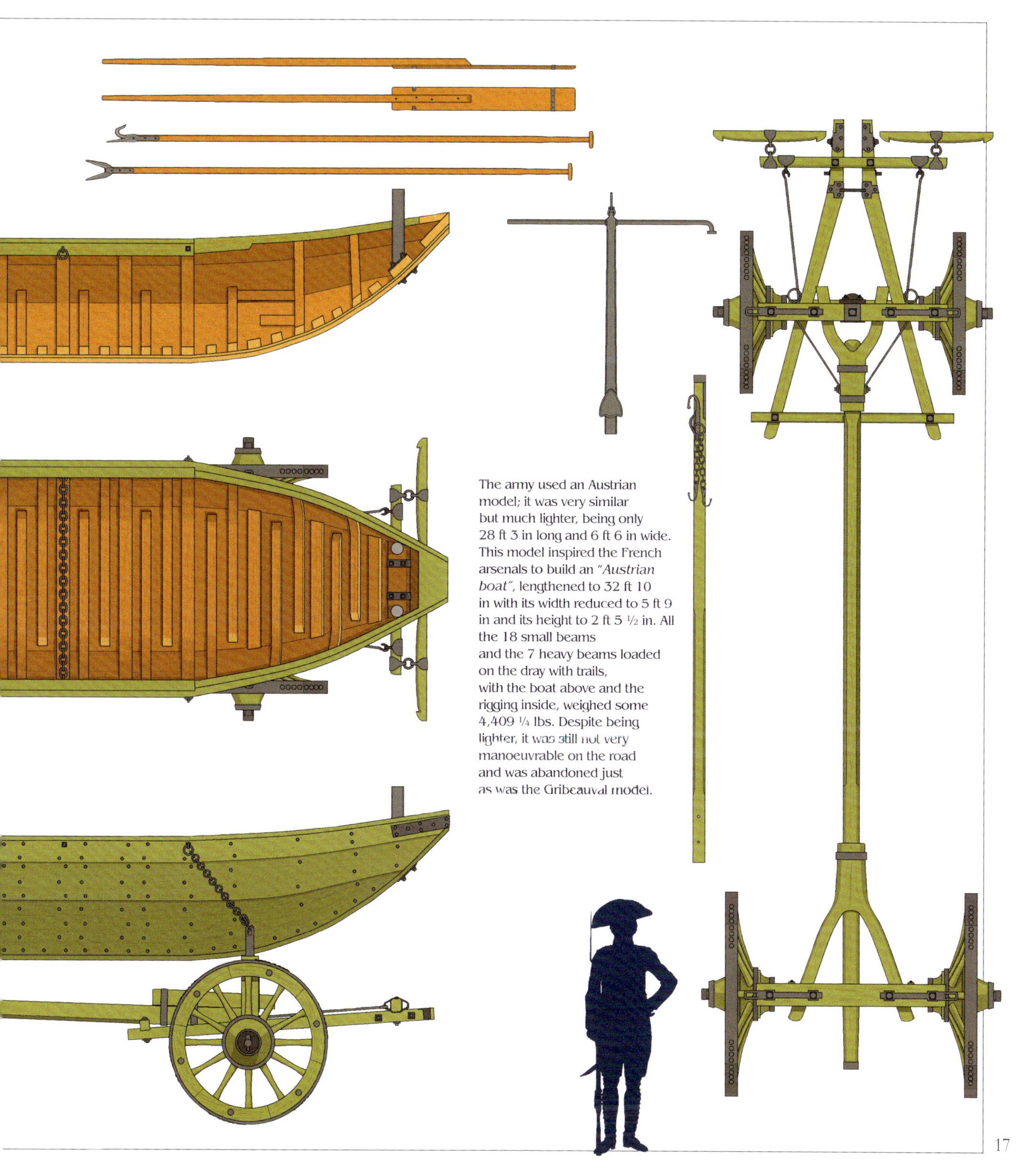

The army used an Austrian model; it was very similar but much lighter, being only 28 ft 3 in long and 6 ft 6 in wide. This model inspired the French arsenals to build an *"Austrian boat"*, lengthened to 32 ft 10 in with its width reduced to 5 ft 9 in and its height to 2 ft 5 ½ in. All the 18 small beams and the 7 heavy beams loaded on the dray with trails, with the boat above and the rigging inside, weighed some 4,409 ¼ lbs. Despite being lighter, it was still not very manoeuvrable on the road and was abandoned just as was the Gribeauval model.

The An-XI (1802-1803) system produced a new model of boat called the Bateau de *l'avant-garde* or the Vanguard Boat to replace the copper pontoon. The vanguard boat had no angles on the sides making it particularly unstable on water. It was 36 1 in long by 5 ft 10 in wide and 2 ft 6 in high. It rested on a dray with litters drawn by six horses; the heavy and small beams were carried on another wagon.

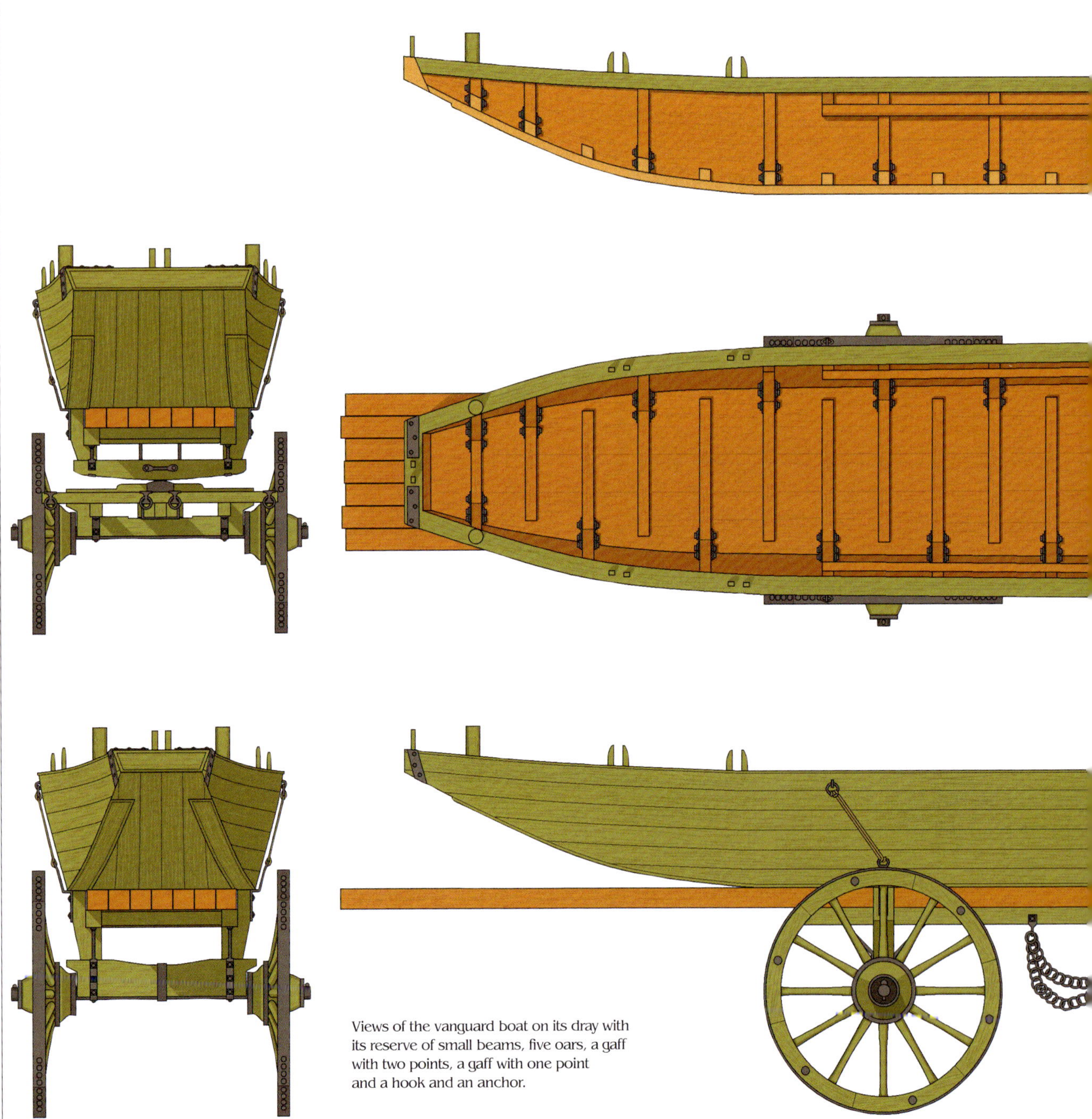

Views of the vanguard boat on its dray with its reserve of small beams, five oars, a gaff with two points, a gaff with one point and a hook and an anchor.

THE VANGUARD BOAT AN XI

A hundred or so of these boats were built at Danzig in 1812 for the Russian Campaign. This model was shortened to 32 ft 10 in, and had a proper angle on the sides with a sharper cutwater. The dray with litter was that of the Gribeauval nacelle or skiff.

COASTAL ARTILLERY

The perpetual, or nearly perpetual, war against England and its navy meant the coastal artillery's role was very important: preventing the Royal Navy from coming too close to the Empire's coast.

While the *Grande Armée* was fighting in Russia or in Prussia, the 23,500 cannon and howitzers of the Coastal Artillery kept watch along the coast for the Empire's security, from the north of Holland to the Mediterranean.

There were guns of all sorts and of all ages. This artillery, fixed by nature and in the end, not used very much, did not need manning by the best gunners in Napoleon's army. Serving the guns therefore fell to the permanent companies or the veterans' companies, men who were unsuited to active service in the regiments of the Line or the Guard.

Although the age of the guns was their main characteristic, some of them were unusual because they were modern or had some innovatory system like the cannon at Cherbourg or at Aix, mounted on swivel pin carriages making reloading faster, or the canon-howitzer set up by Colonel de Villantroys, which had an effective range of almost 4,375 yds.

THE COASTGUARD GUNNERS

It was the decree dated 8 Prairial An XI (28 May 1803) that created and organised the 100 coastguard companies, split up among the artillery directorates. There were 114 companies six years later (new companies had been created as the years went by in le Havre, in the Alpes Maritimes, in Liguria, Tuscany, Corsica and Antwerp). The number of companies varied in each directorate.

A Coastal Battalion Commander Adjudant was in charge of the proper running of the companies. He had two assistants in the directorates in which more than ten companies had been set up. Organising these companies needed a quartermaster in charge of accounting.

THE COASTGUARD GUNNERS COMPANY

— 1 captain
— 1 lieutenant
— 1 sergeant-major
— Main magazine guard
— 4 sergeants
— 8 corporals
— 8 appointees
— 96 gunners
— 2 drummers

Total: 121 artillerymen

THE 16 ARTILLERY DIRECTORATES

Antwerp,
Lille,
Saint-Omer,
Le Havre,
Cherbourg,
Brest,
Nantes,
La Rochelle,
Bayonne,
Perpignan,
Montpellier,
Toulon,
Antibes,
Corsica,
Genoa
and Tuscany

For each artillery directorate where the gunner companies were set up, there was also a Coastal Battalion Commander Adjudant who was in charge of the service. In the directorates where there were more than 10 companies, this adjudant would have two assistants. There was also a quartermaster in each directorate in charge of the accounts. Half the coastguard gunner officers came from the corps, a third from the artillery of the Line and the rest from the Navy artillery after 1804.

28 companies of permanent coastguard gunners were created in 1804 as well as the coastguard gunner companies. This number rose to 30 in 1808. They were National Guard units and the companies' make up was the same as the coastguard gunners.

These companies' theoretical strength at the height of the Empire was 228 officers and 13,566 NCOs and gunners for the Coastguards, and 60 officers and 3,570 NCOs and gunners for the Permanent Companies. As one can judge, this was hardly a force to be ignored.

THE NAVAL GUNNERS

In 1814 the Naval Gunners at Cherbourg and Toulon were organised into 8 companies (four in each town). Each comprised a Captain CO, a first lieutenant, two second lieutenants, a sergeant-major, four sergeants, a furrier, four corporals, four artificers, 24 first gunners, 80 second gunners and two drummers. They served mainly the sea front batteries – the coastal batteries.

(Continued on page 32)

THE GRIBEAUVAL SYSTEM NACELLE

The nacelles, or skiffs, were used by the pontoneers when setting up a bridge, for bringing up the ropes and the anchors. There were different types of skiffs, the smallest measuring 13 ft 1 ½ in ft to the Gribeauval model measuring 28 ft long, 3 ft 4 in wide and 1 ft 4 in high.

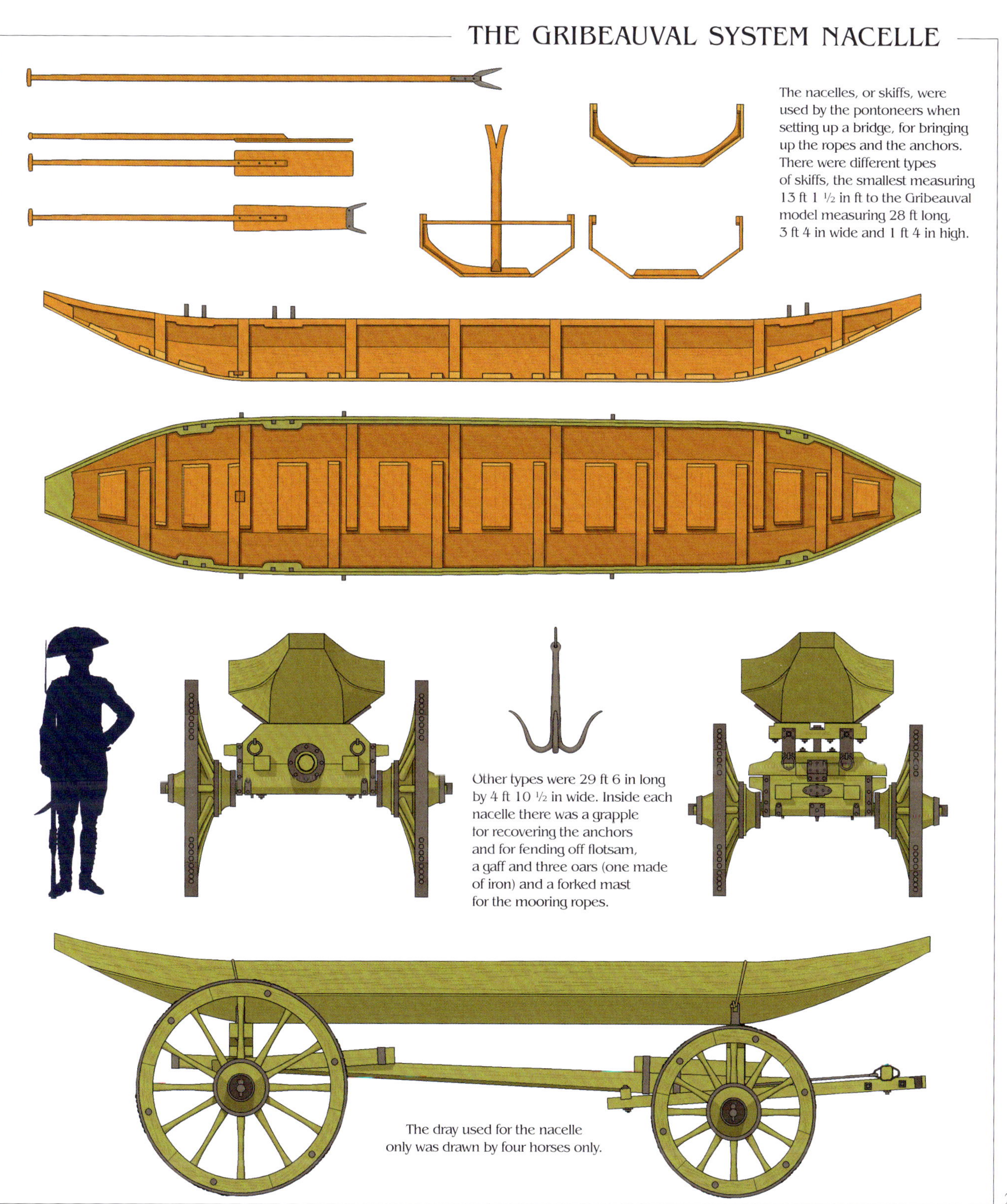

Other types were 29 ft 6 in long by 4 ft 10 ½ in wide. Inside each nacelle there was a grapple for recovering the anchors and for fending off flotsam, a gaff and three oars (one made of iron) and a forked mast for the mooring ropes.

The dray used for the nacelle only was drawn by four horses only.

THE FORGE AND THE TEAM WAGON

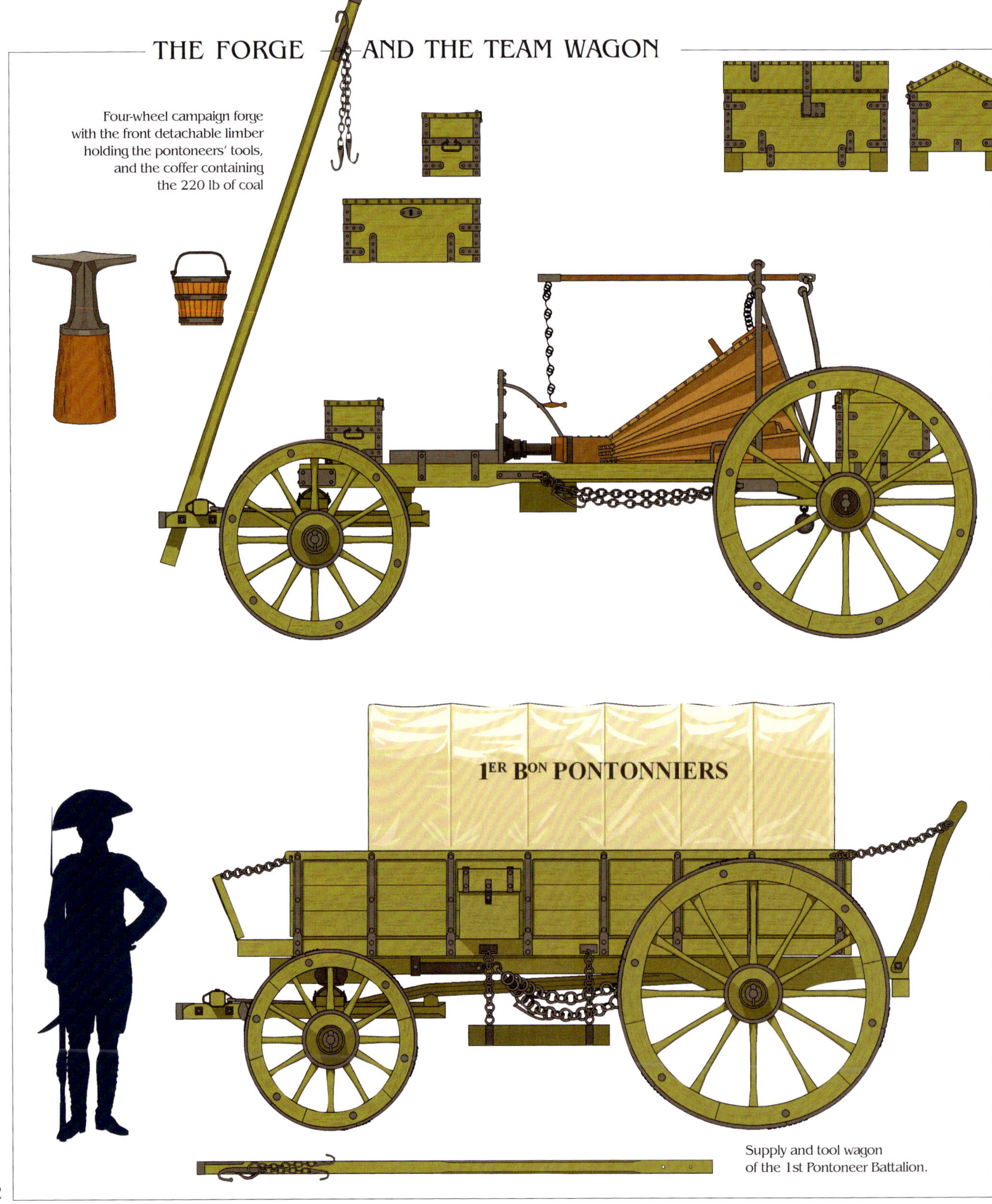

Four-wheel campaign forge with the front detachable limber holding the pontoneers' tools, and the coffer containing the 220 lb of coal

Supply and tool wagon of the 1st Pontoneer Battalion.

THE PILE DRIVER

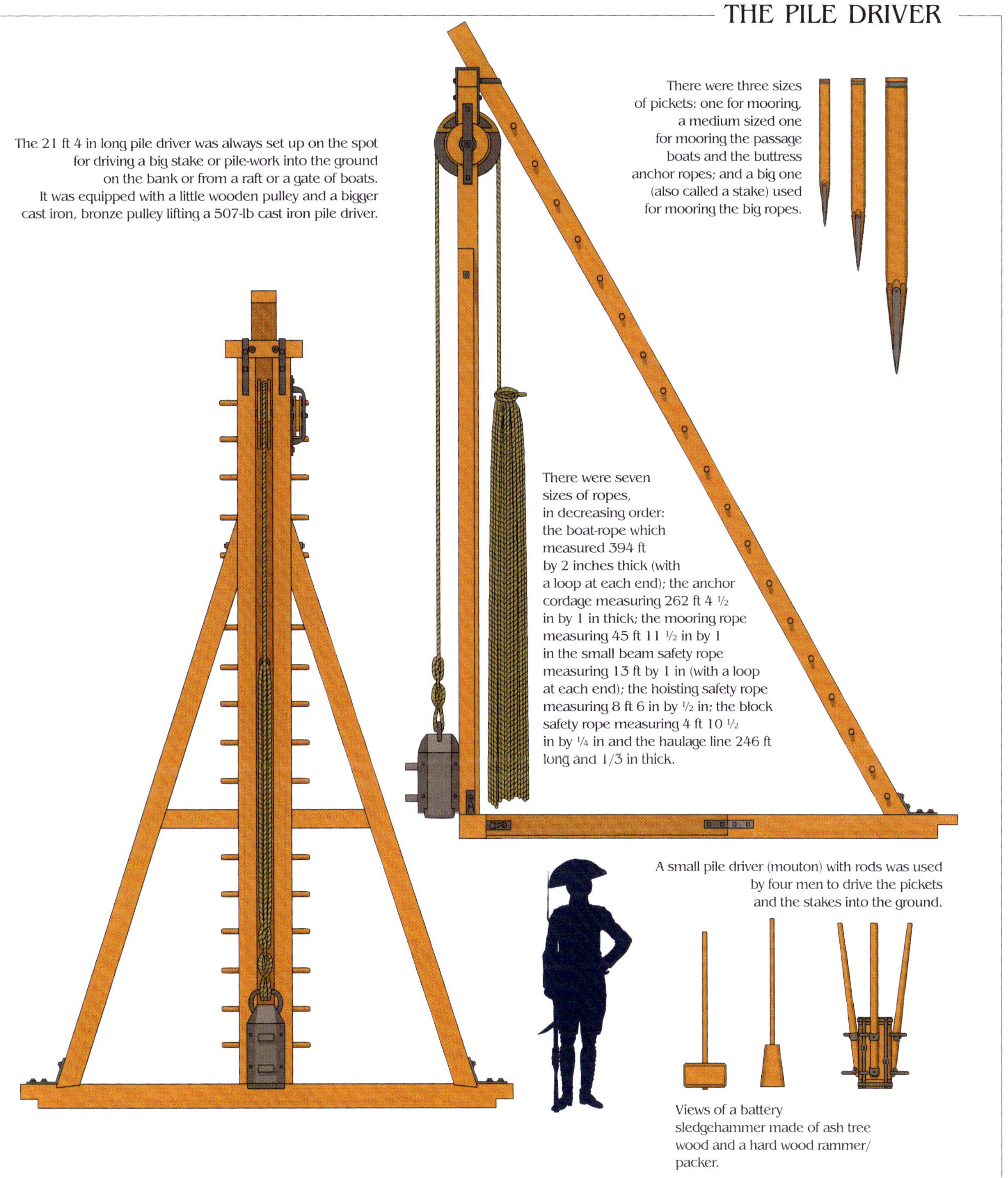

The 21 ft 4 in long pile driver was always set up on the spot for driving a big stake or pile-work into the ground on the bank or from a raft or a gate of boats. It was equipped with a little wooden pulley and a bigger cast iron, bronze pulley lifting a 507-lb cast iron pile driver.

There were three sizes of pickets: one for mooring, a medium sized one for mooring the passage boats and the buttress anchor ropes; and a big one (also called a stake) used for mooring the big ropes.

There were seven sizes of ropes, in decreasing order: the boat-rope which measured 394 ft by 2 inches thick (with a loop at each end); the anchor cordage measuring 262 ft 4 ½ in by 1 in thick; the mooring rope measuring 45 ft 11 ½ in by 1 in the small beam safety rope measuring 13 ft by 1 in (with a loop at each end); the hoisting safety rope measuring 8 ft 6 in by ½ in; the block safety rope measuring 4 ft 10 ½ in by ¼ in and the haulage line 246 ft long and 1/3 in thick.

A small pile driver (mouton) with rods was used by four men to drive the pickets and the stakes into the ground.

Views of a battery sledgehammer made of ash tree wood and a hard wood rammer/packer.

THE RIGGIN AND TACKLE

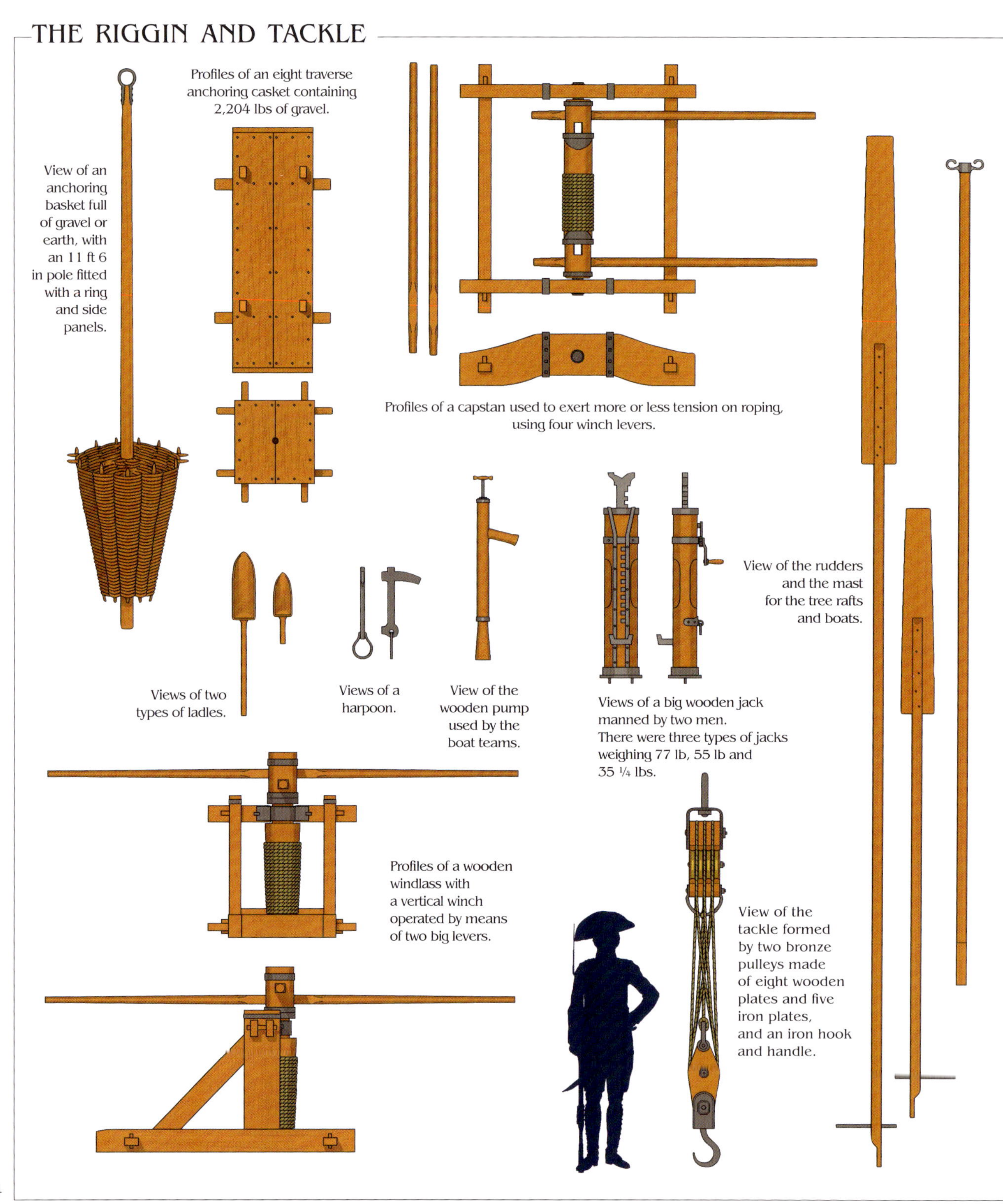

THE BOAT BRIDGE AND THE PONTOON

Bridging with a string of boats using the Gribeauval System remained the most common way of throwing a bridge across a deep, wide and fast-moving river. Each boat was set at most 21 ft 4 in from its neighbour from the middle outwards. The boats could take a load of up to 8,818 lbs by reducing this gap. The bridge was moored to the bank abutments and anchored along its entire length by a nacelle. Ideally, two boat bridges were built to allow traffic in both directions. Any type of boat was used and all were suitable for forming a boat bridge.

In certain circumstances, a so-called "conversion" bridge was built along the first bank and afterwards launched across to the other side.

In order to facilitate all the construction manoeuvres or to fold the bridge back, the boats, anchors and rigging were numbered in order, which was used starting from the first buttress.

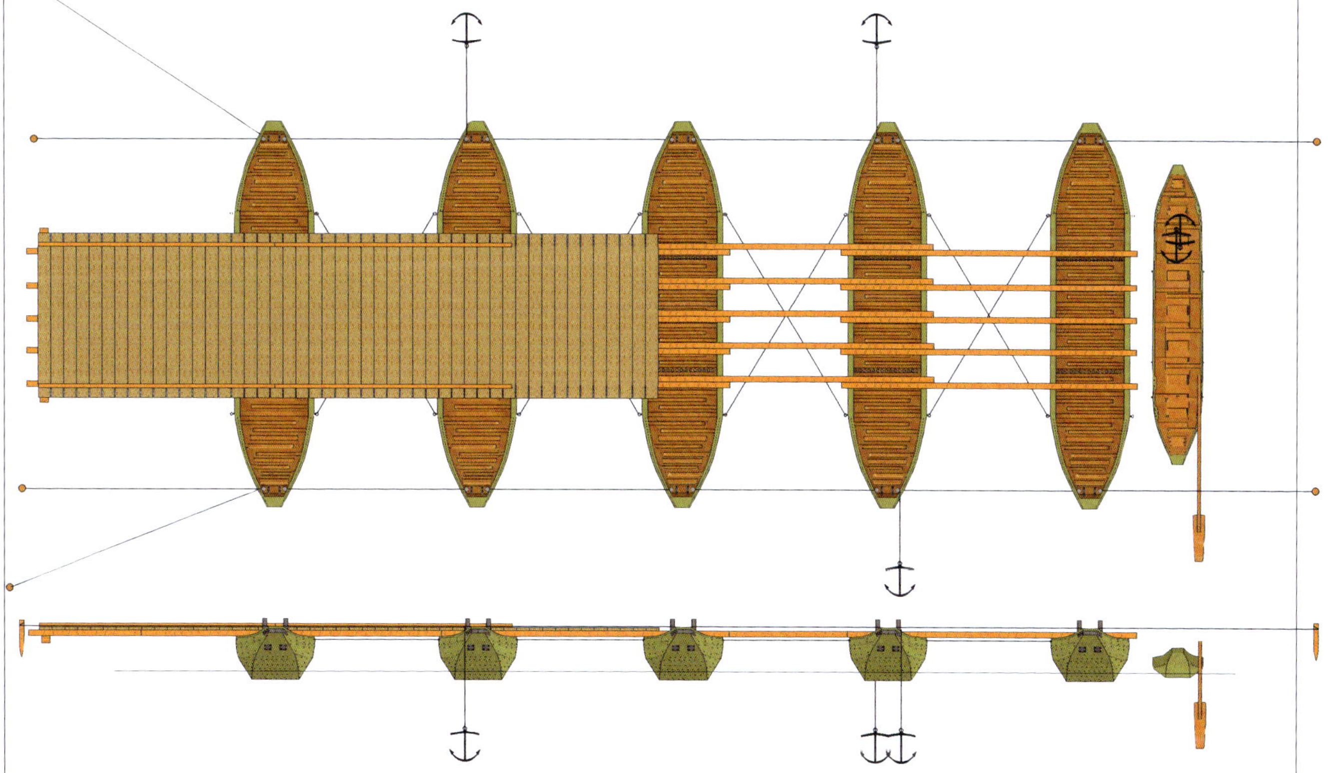

he Gribeauval pontoon was too fragile to take a load of more than s despite the pontoons being just ten feet apart. Moreover the pontoons could only be set up from one bank to the other, over a distance of 165 yd or less and then only in a weak current. The pontoon was unsuited to navigation and could only be moved up by road.

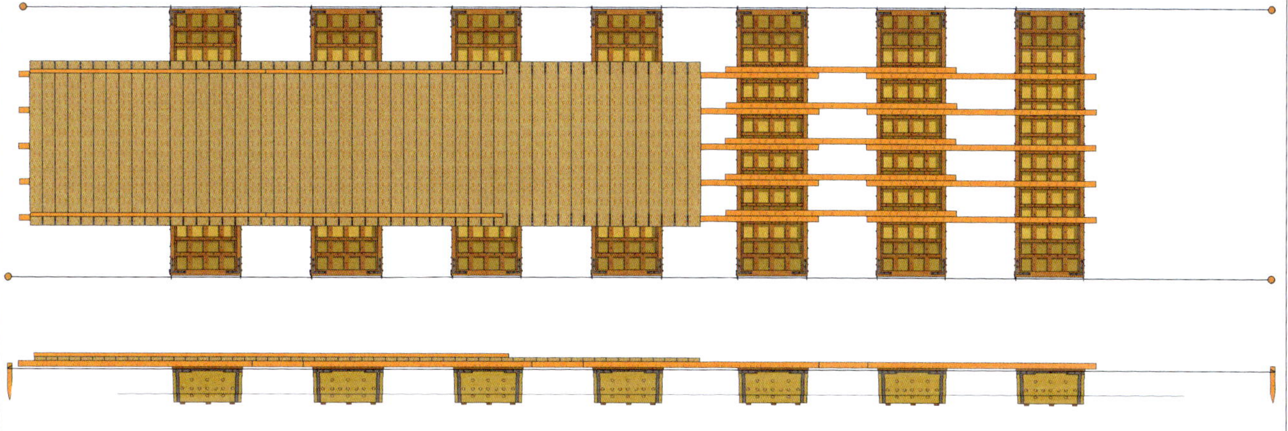

BRIDGES IN SECTIONS AND IN GATES

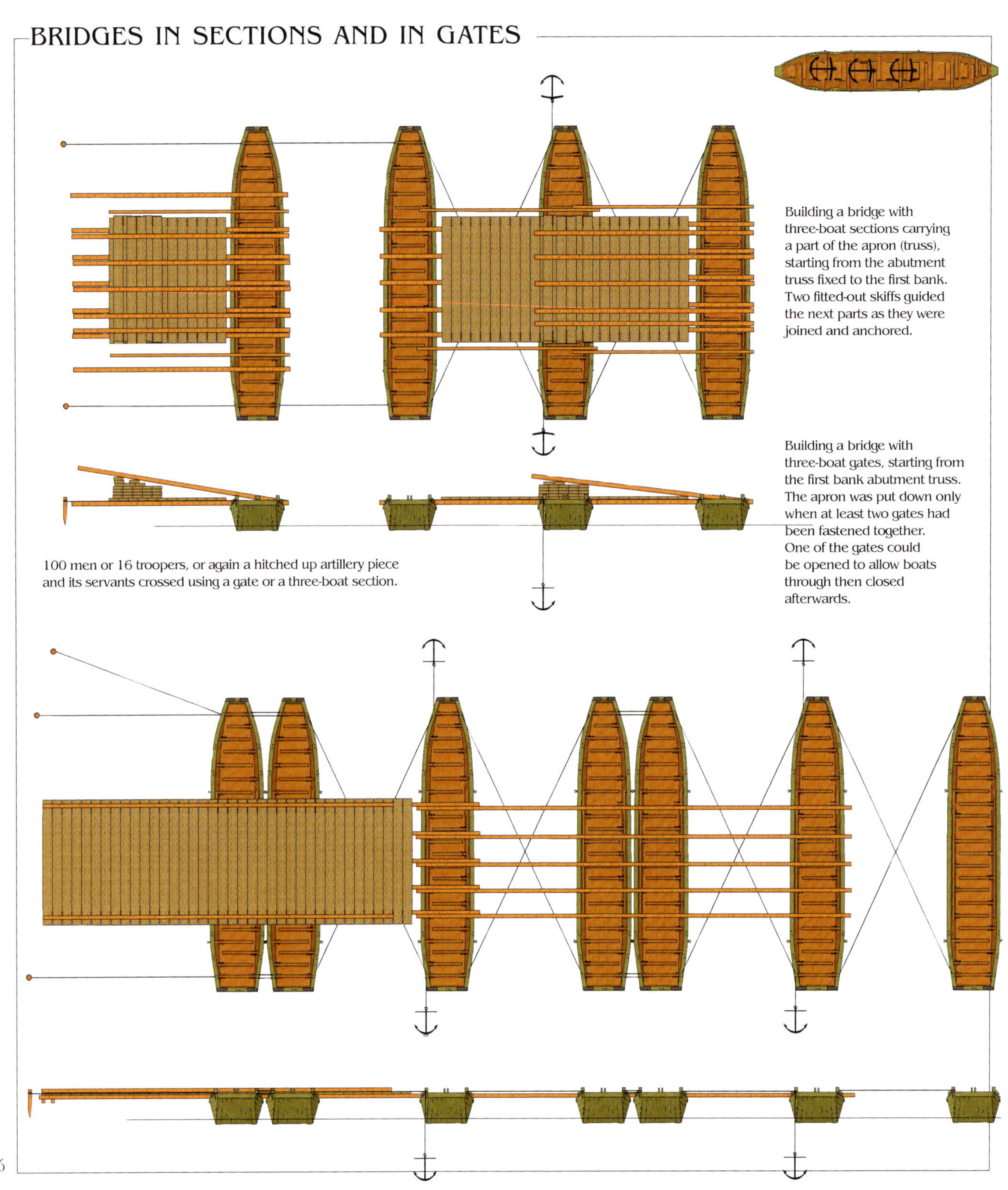

Building a bridge with three-boat sections carrying a part of the apron (truss), starting from the abutment truss fixed to the first bank. Two fitted-out skiffs guided the next parts as they were joined and anchored.

Building a bridge with three-boat gates, starting from the first bank abutment truss. The apron was put down only when at least two gates had been fastened together. One of the gates could be opened to allow boats through then closed afterwards.

100 men or 16 troopers, or again a hitched up artillery piece and its servants crossed using a gate or a three-boat section.

FOUR-LEG TRESTLE BRIDGES

Trestle bridges were set up to replace the team train bridges which had not been able to keep up with the campaigning army. The trestles were set up by eight men every 13 ft from one of the bank abutments. This type of rapid construction was only used across a river which was not more than 6 ft 6 in deep.

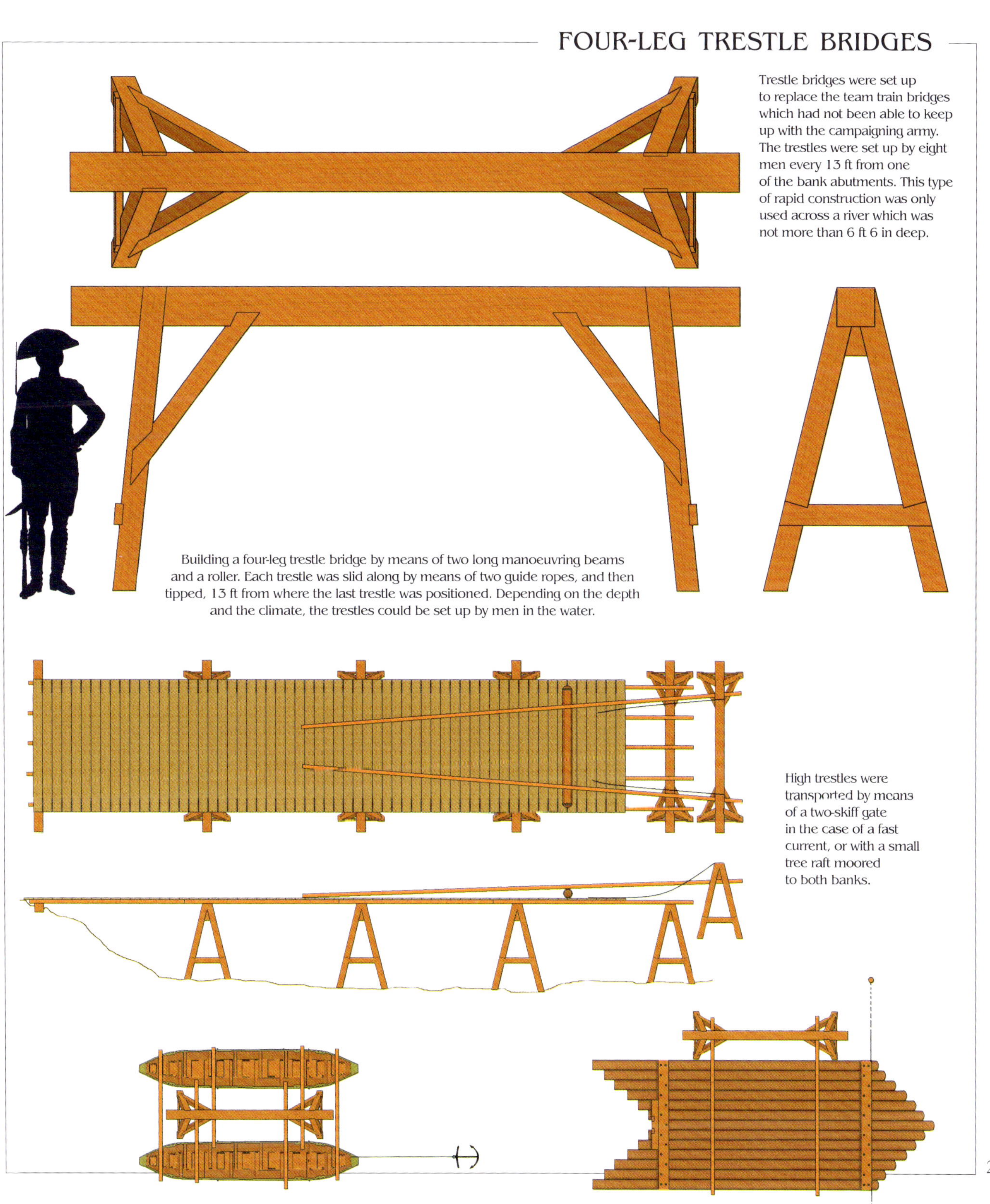

Building a four-leg trestle bridge by means of two long manoeuvring beams and a roller. Each trestle was slid along by means of two guide ropes, and then tipped, 13 ft from where the last trestle was positioned. Depending on the depth and the climate, the trestles could be set up by men in the water.

High trestles were transported by means of a two-skiff gate in the case of a fast current, or with a small tree raft moored to both banks.

TRESTLE BRIDGES WITH TWO IMPROVISED LEGS

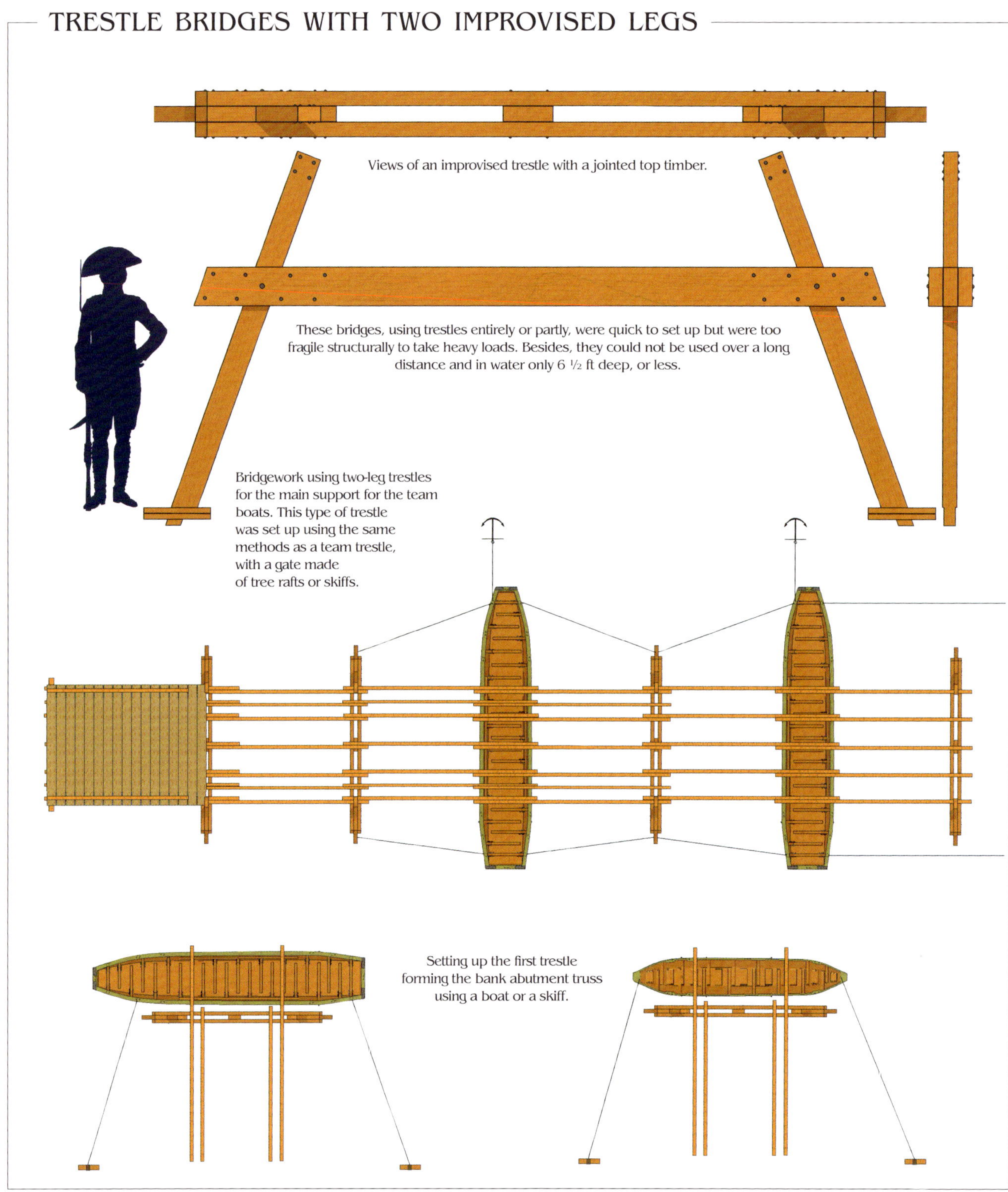

Views of an improvised trestle with a jointed top timber.

These bridges, using trestles entirely or partly, were quick to set up but were too fragile structurally to take heavy loads. Besides, they could not be used over a long distance and in water only 6 ½ ft deep, or less.

Bridgework using two-leg trestles for the main support for the team boats. This type of trestle was set up using the same methods as a team trestle, with a gate made of tree rafts or skiffs.

Setting up the first trestle forming the bank abutment truss using a boat or a skiff.

PILE-WORKS BRIDGE

Pile-work bridges were generally built by the Engineer sappers, in the army rear for communications purposes. The pontoneers themselves used this type of construction for freeing a team bridge.

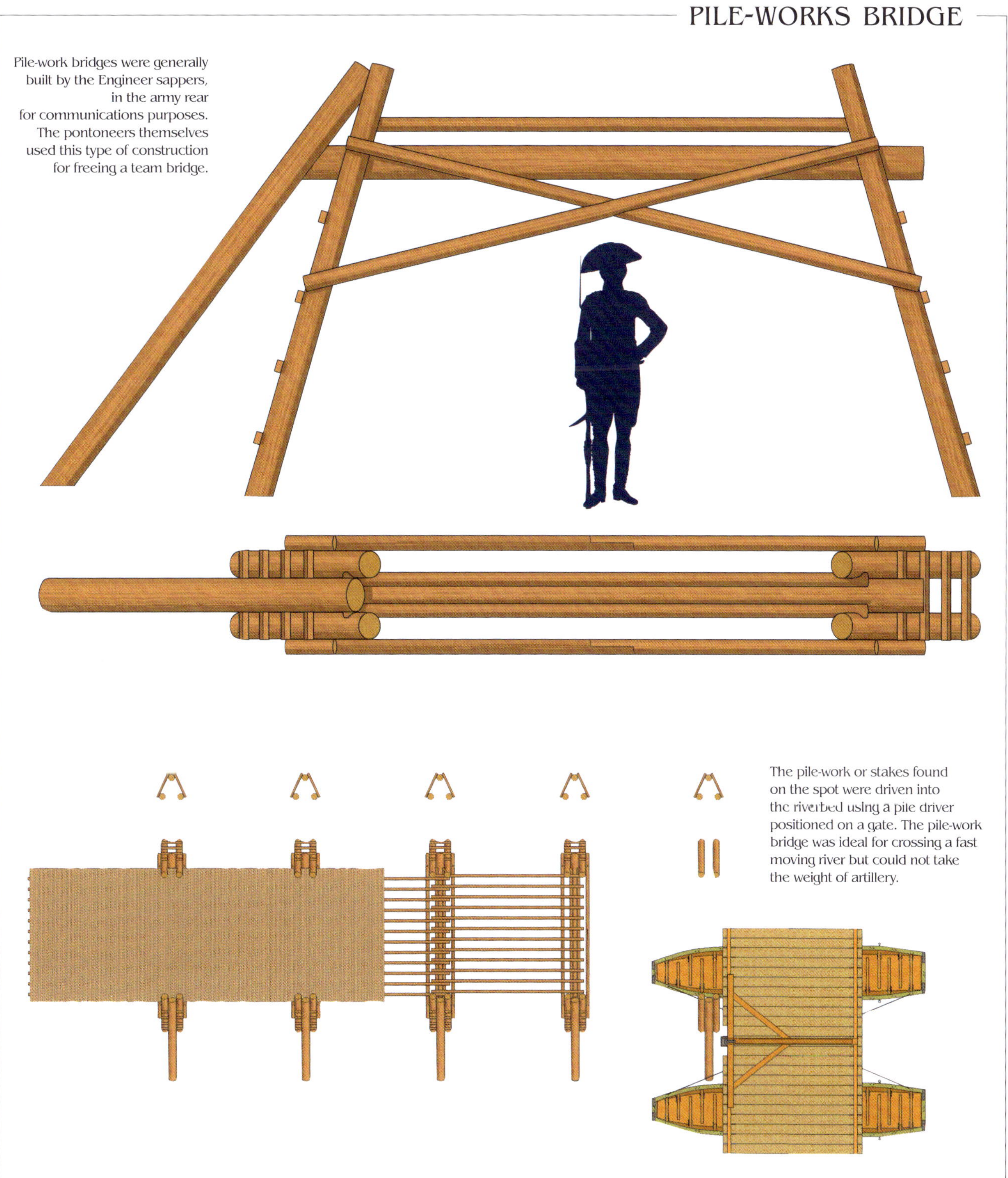

The pile-work or stakes found on the spot were driven into the riverbed using a pile driver positioned on a gate. The pile-work bridge was ideal for crossing a fast moving river but could not take the weight of artillery.

THE MOVING BRIDGE AND THE BOAT TRAIN

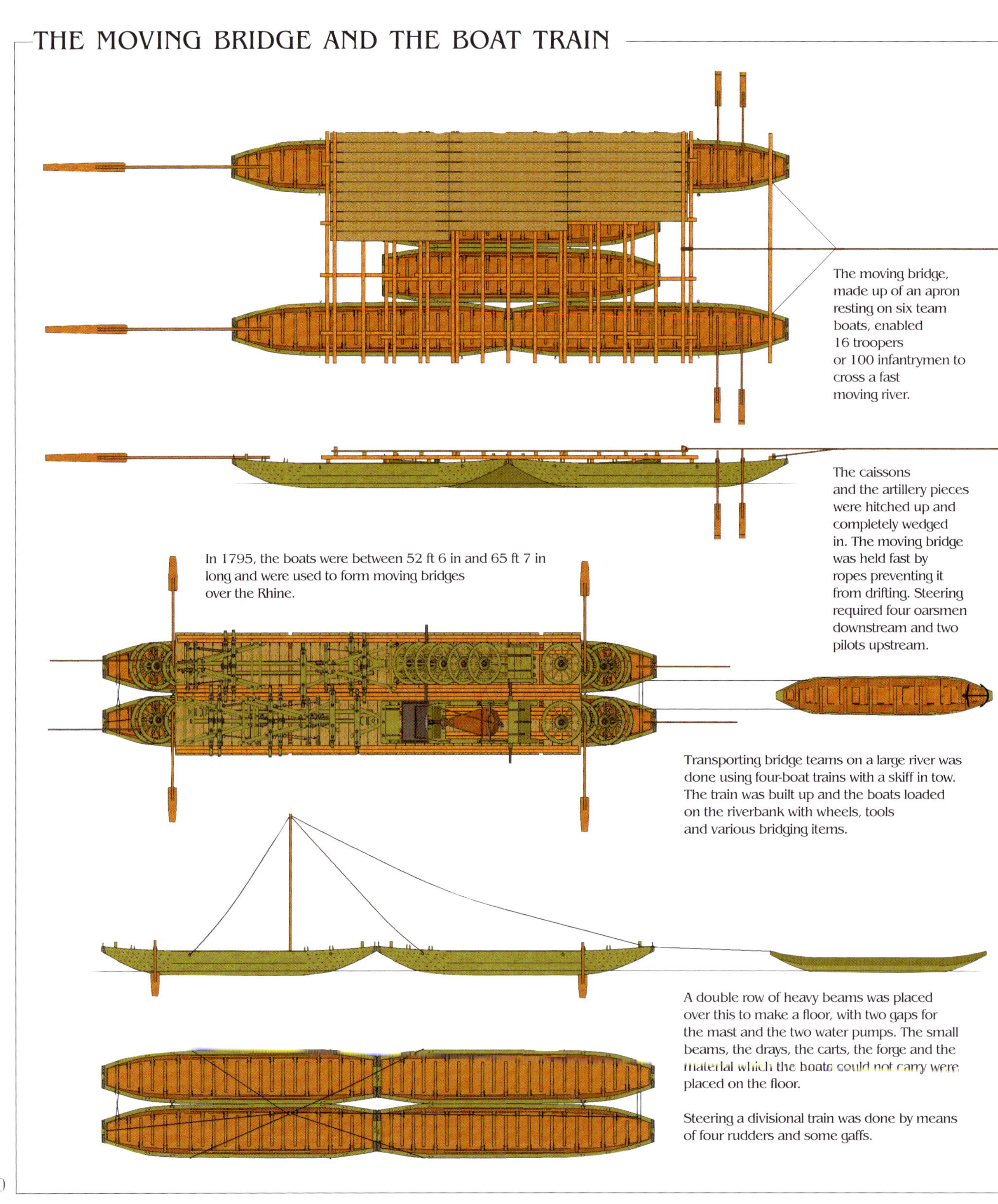

The moving bridge, made up of an apron resting on six team boats, enabled 16 troopers or 100 infantrymen to cross a fast moving river.

The caissons and the artillery pieces were hitched up and completely wedged in. The moving bridge was held fast by ropes preventing it from drifting. Steering required four oarsmen downstream and two pilots upstream.

In 1795, the boats were between 52 ft 6 in and 65 ft 7 in long and were used to form moving bridges over the Rhine.

Transporting bridge teams on a large river was done using four-boat trains with a skiff in tow. The train was built up and the boats loaded on the riverbank with wheels, tools and various bridging items.

A double row of heavy beams was placed over this to make a floor, with two gaps for the mast and the two water pumps. The small beams, the drays, the carts, the forge and the material which the boats could not carry were placed on the floor.

Steering a divisional train was done by means of four rudders and some gaffs.

If there were no boats available tree rafts were made from wood found on the spot. Almost always built using the boat bridge method, the gates could be made with two half-rafts.

Each raft was brought up by five men equipped with four gaffs and a rudder, and anchored using a skiff. Raft bridges could only be formed on slow-moving rivers.

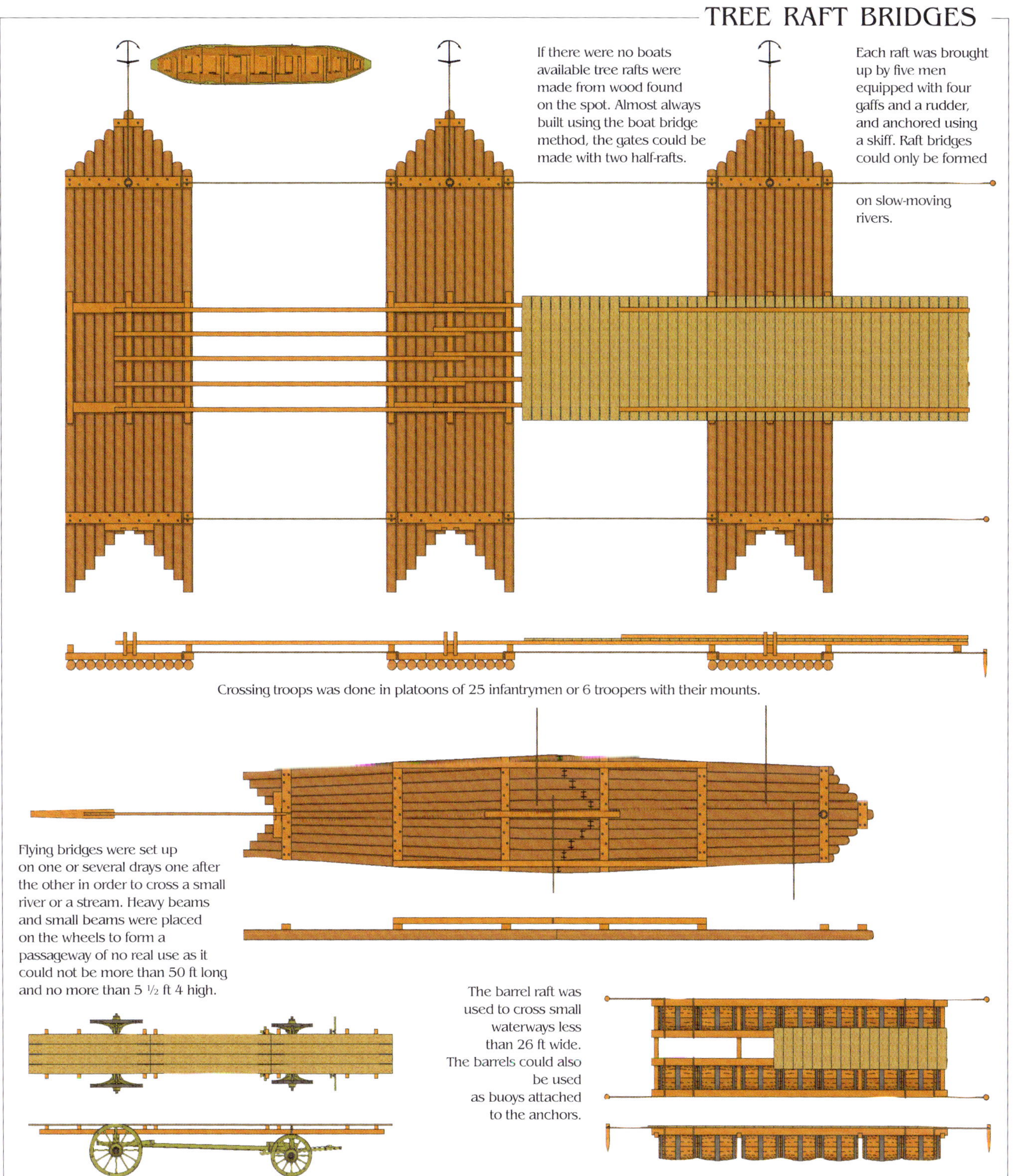

Crossing troops was done in platoons of 25 infantrymen or 6 troopers with their mounts.

Flying bridges were set up on one or several drays one after the other in order to cross a small river or a stream. Heavy beams and small beams were placed on the wheels to form a passageway of no real use as it could not be more than 50 ft long and no more than 5 ½ ft 4 high.

The barrel raft was used to cross small waterways less than 26 ft wide. The barrels could also be used as buoys attached to the anchors.

GUNNERS FOR THE COLONIES

On 10 February 1808 a decree planned the setting up of two companies of Gunners *"young and full of goodwill"* for the Colonies. These men were to be recruited on a voluntary basis in the Coastguard Gunner Companies *"from Lorient to Brest"*. The *Première compagnie de canonniers des colonies* was formed at Lorient and the *2e compagnie de canonniers des colonies* on the Island of Aix.

Each company was made up of a captain, a first lieutenant, a second lieutenant, a sergeant-major, fours sergeants, a corporal-furrier, eight corporals, 140 gunners and two drummers.

THE LILLE PERMANENT GUNNERS

This famous corps was created on 2 May 1483 and took the name of the *Lille Confrèrie des canonniers et couleuvriniers*, or the *Confrérie de Sainte-Barbe* and defended its ramparts ever since. It was one of the oldest artillery units in Europe.

In 1791, it was attached to the National Guard. On 13 FructidorAn XI (31 August 1803) as a tribute to the extraordinary valour of the gunners and their commanding officer, Captain Ovigneur, during the siege in 1792, Napoleon organised them into a two-company battalion, separate from the National Guard.

The headquarters rather classically included a commander in chief, a quartermaster treasurer, and a standard-bearer. Each company comprised a captain, a first-lieutenant, a second-lieutenant, a sergeant-major, two sergeants, a corporal-furrier, four corporals, four sappers, two artificers, two workers, four gunners first class, 35 to 39 gunners second-class, and a drummer. The Lille Permanent Gunners distinguished themselves in all the conflicts of the 19th and 20th Centuries.

THE VETERAN GUNNERS

On 20 Vendémiaire An XI (12 October 1802) a decree increased the number of Veteran Gunner companies from 13 to 14, and assigned 25 more men to each of them. The number of companies reached 18 in 1803. Each company comprised a first captain, a second captain, a sergeant-major, three sergeants, a furrier, six corporals, 60 gunners, and two drummers. The decree dated 27 Floréal An XIII (17 May 1805) organised once and for all the Corps of "Imperial Veterans" into 100 companies of which 25 were Veteran Gunners.

THE TEAM TRAINS

The instructions dated 28 Nivôse An III (17 January 1795), insisting on the primordial role of military transport, laid down its main duties. In 1803, the administration sent out regulations which were supposed to define the role, capabilities, rights and duties of the *"military teams assigned to the service of supplies and ambulances, and to transporting items for the camps or the armies."*

The teams, which were not yet the Team Train, were organised into brigades. The transport service was divided at this point into quite distinct services.

- Supplies, ambulances, camp items.
- Caissons following the corps and the generals
- The Pool service (transport in general)
- The artillery teams

Two civilian companies dealt with the transport: the House of Breidt, in charge of the *Grande Armée*; and the Gayde Company for the Army of Italy's transport (see opposite).

This set up was far from satisfactory and turned out

(Continued on page 64)

1. A commercial boat bridge was built using the same method as the boat bridge with equipment requisitioned on the spot. Being unequal, the boats were arranged under the bridge by size starting from the first abutment. Scaffolding made of traverses, or trestles, was placed in the boats whose sides were too low down to keep the apron level. The boat was anchored with earth baskets and anchoring caskets.

2. A ferry was set up (without bank abutment trusses) with a cable fixed to the bank at one end and pulled by men in the ferry. The cable passed through a pulley placed on the mountings of the ferry. When the ferry crossed, a skiff recovered the cable to fasten it to the other side, and so on. The ferry consisting of coupled boats could carry 60 infantrymen or 8 troopers and their mounts. In the same manner a boat, a raft or a skiff could be used as a ferry, with a mast raised in the embarkation.

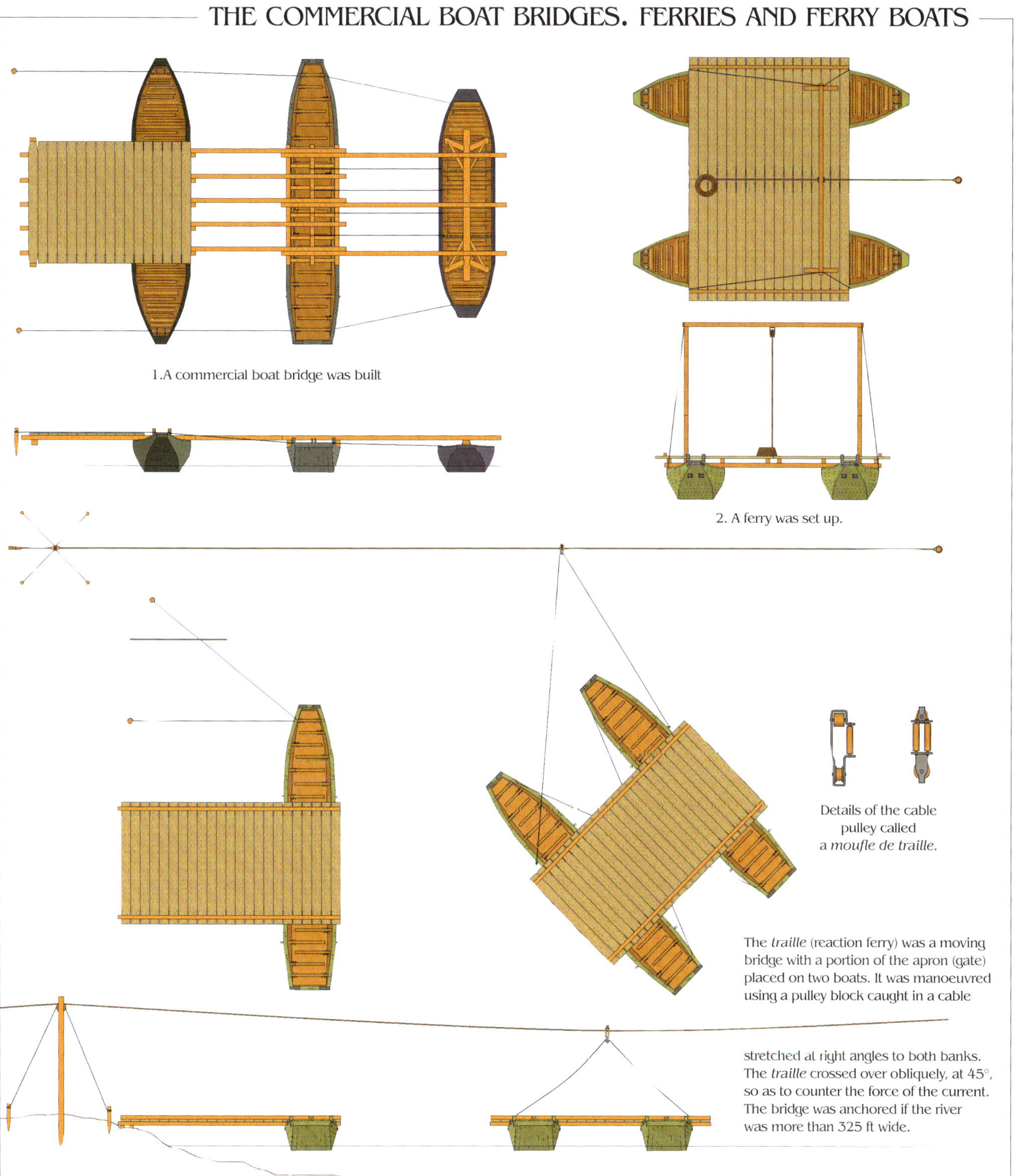

1.A commercial boat bridge was built

2. A ferry was set up.

Details of the cable pulley called a *moufle de traille.*

The *traille* (reaction ferry) was a moving bridge with a portion of the apron (gate) placed on two boats. It was manoeuvred using a pulley block caught in a cable stretched at right angles to both banks. The *traille* crossed over obliquely, at 45°, so as to counter the force of the current. The bridge was anchored if the river was more than 325 ft wide.

THE GRIBEAUVAL 8-INCH SIEGE HOWITZER

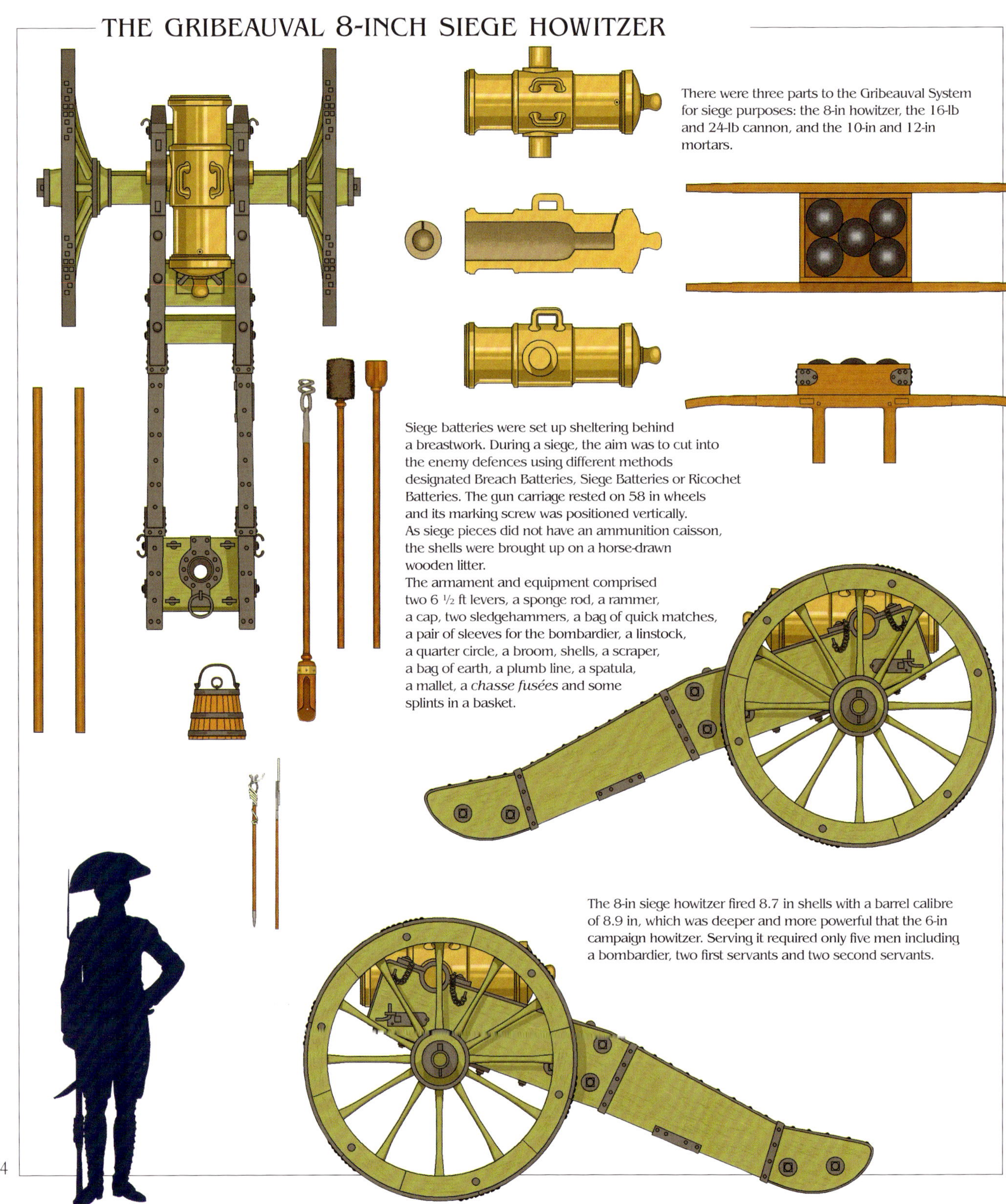

There were three parts to the Gribeauval System for siege purposes: the 8-in howitzer, the 16-lb and 24-lb cannon, and the 10-in and 12-in mortars.

Siege batteries were set up sheltering behind a breastwork. During a siege, the aim was to cut into the enemy defences using different methods designated Breach Batteries, Siege Batteries or Ricochet Batteries. The gun carriage rested on 58 in wheels and its marking screw was positioned vertically. As siege pieces did not have an ammunition caisson, the shells were brought up on a horse-drawn wooden litter.
The armament and equipment comprised two 6 ½ ft levers, a sponge rod, a rammer, a cap, two sledgehammers, a bag of quick matches, a pair of sleeves for the bombardier, a linstock, a quarter circle, a broom, shells, a scraper, a bag of earth, a plumb line, a spatula, a mallet, a *chasse fusées* and some splints in a basket.

The 8-in siege howitzer fired 8.7 in shells with a barrel calibre of 8.9 in, which was deeper and more powerful that the 6-in campaign howitzer. Serving it required only five men including a bombardier, two first servants and two second servants.

THE GRIBEAUVAL 16-LB SIEGE GUN

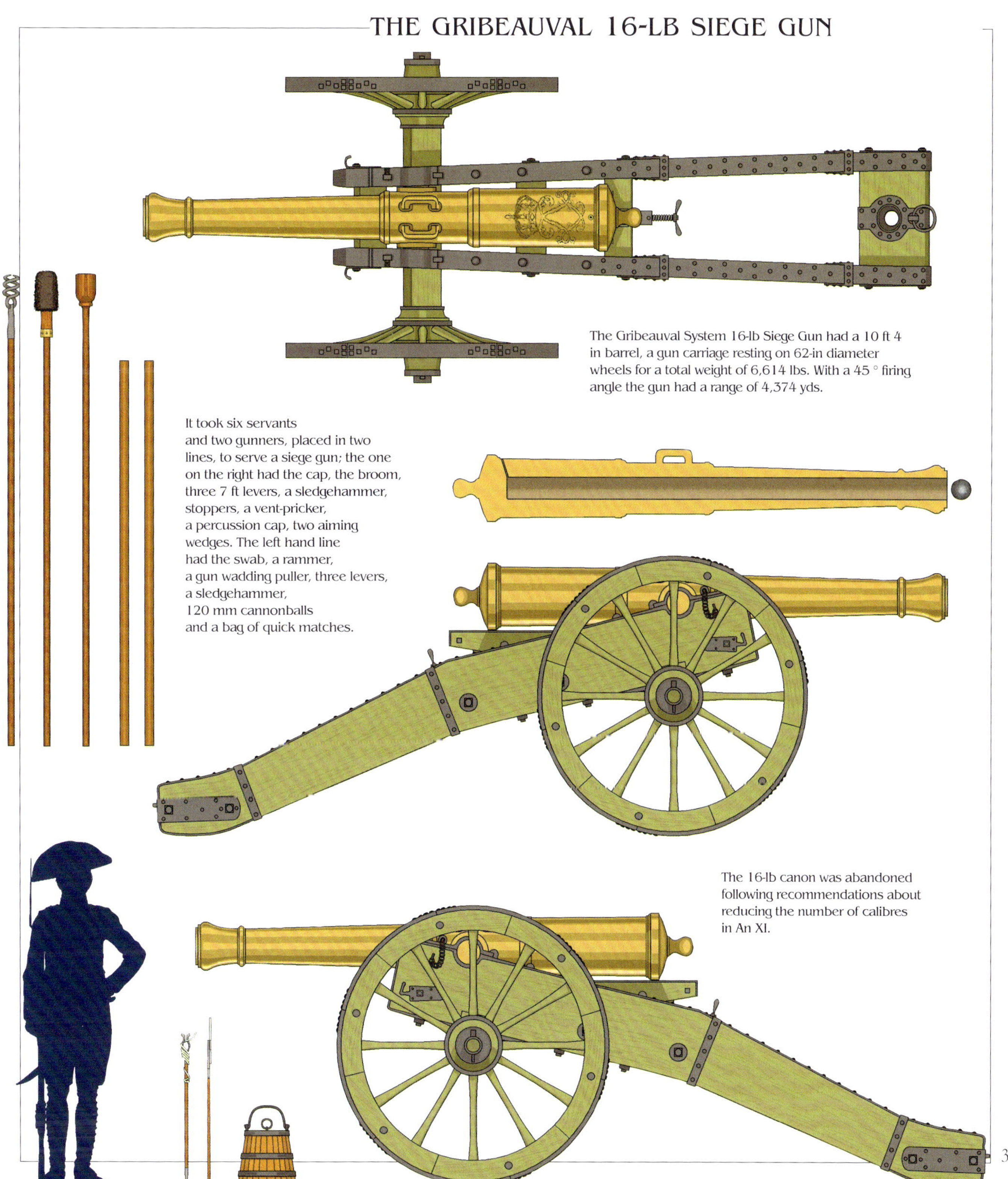

The Gribeauval System 16-lb Siege Gun had a 10 ft 4 in barrel, a gun carriage resting on 62-in diameter wheels for a total weight of 6,614 lbs. With a 45 ° firing angle the gun had a range of 4,374 yds.

It took six servants and two gunners, placed in two lines, to serve a siege gun; the one on the right had the cap, the broom, three 7 ft levers, a sledgehammer, stoppers, a vent-pricker, a percussion cap, two aiming wedges. The left hand line had the swab, a rammer, a gun wadding puller, three levers, a sledgehammer, 120 mm cannonballs and a bag of quick matches.

The 16-lb canon was abandoned following recommendations about reducing the number of calibres in An XI.

THE GRIBEAUVAL 24-LB SIEGE GUN

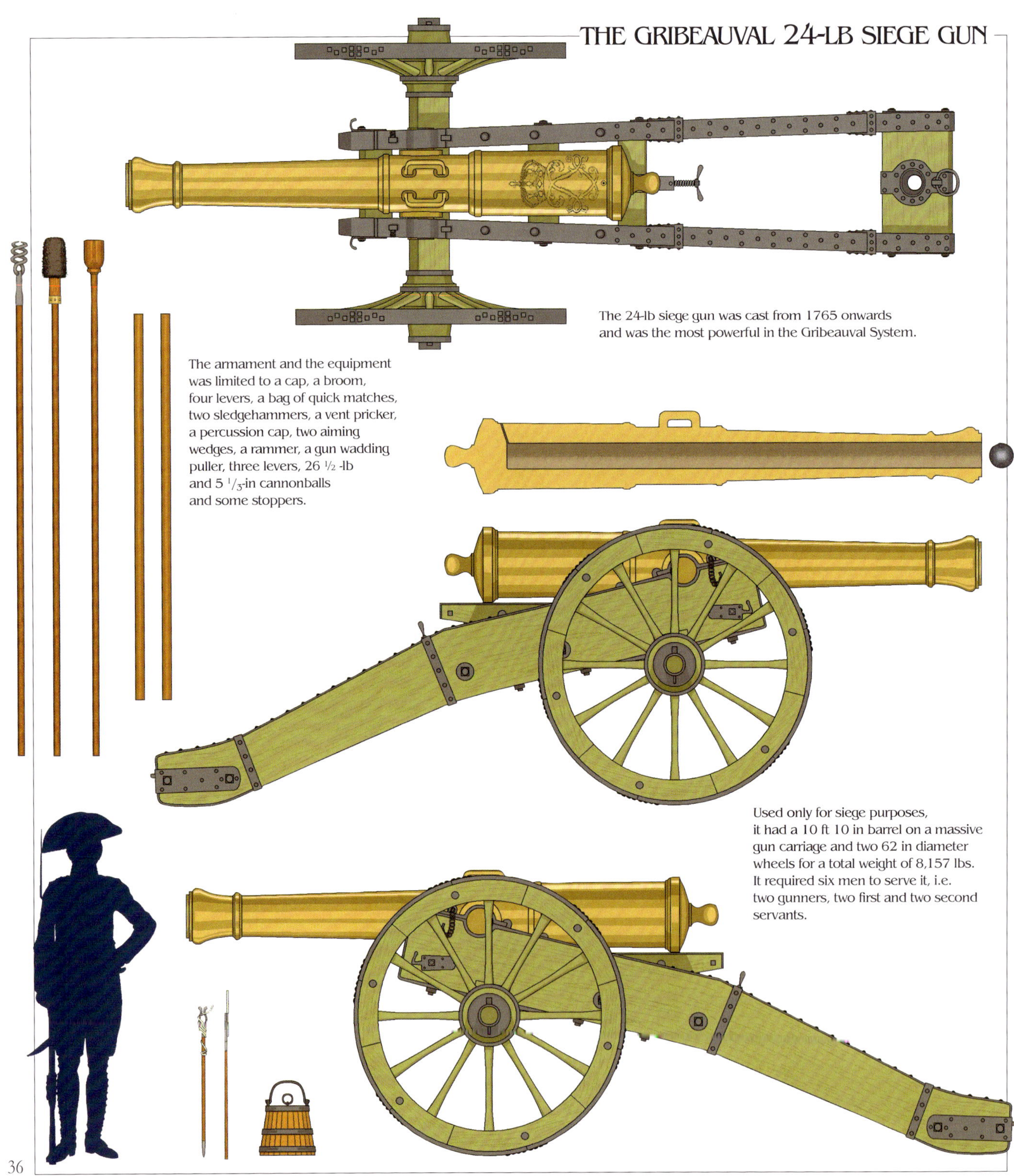

The 24-lb siege gun was cast from 1765 onwards and was the most powerful in the Gribeauval System.

The armament and the equipment was limited to a cap, a broom, four levers, a bag of quick matches, two sledgehammers, a vent pricker, a percussion cap, two aiming wedges, a rammer, a gun wadding puller, three levers, 26 ½ -lb and 5 $^{1}/_{3}$-in cannonballs and some stoppers.

Used only for siege purposes, it had a 10 ft 10 in barrel on a massive gun carriage and two 62 in diameter wheels for a total weight of 8,157 lbs. It required six men to serve it, i.e. two gunners, two first and two second servants.

THE CYLINDRICAL CHAMBER GRIBEAUVAL MORTAR

The first Gribeauval System mortars used a cylindrical chamber which prevented the bomb from being wedged in properly. Since the blast caused shocks when the mortar was fired, the servants limited themselves to 30 shots per 24 hours. The mortar hurled its black powder-filled bomb in a curved trajectory over an obstacle, ready to explode at a given moment calculated by the artificer. Field artillery used 8-, 10- and 12-inch mortars; strongholds used 8-, 10- and 12-inch mortars, coastal batteries 10- and 12-inch mortars and the siege artillery used 8-, 10- and 12-inch mortars.

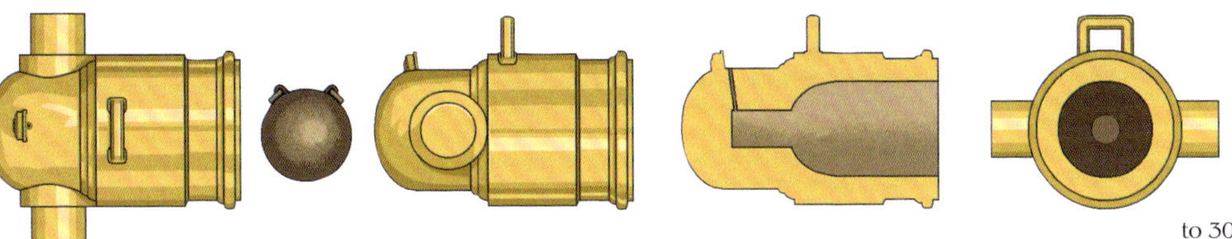

12-in, 35 ½ in long, cylindrical mortar weighing 2,866 lbs with a maximum range of 4,934 yards using a 159-lb bomb and a 3,086-lb iron gun carriage.

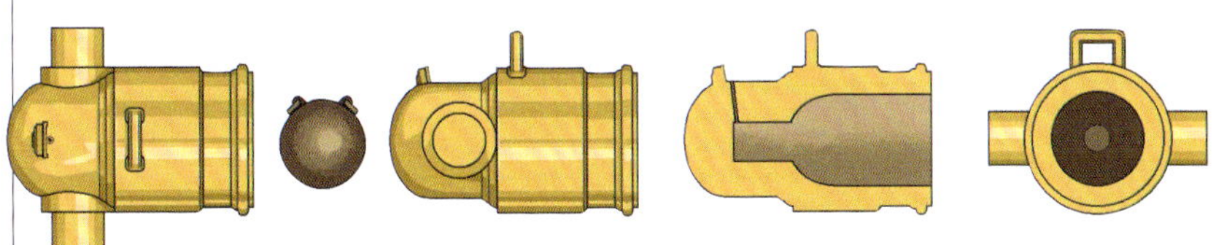

10-in, 29-in long, cylindrical mortar weighing 1,720 lbs with a maximum range of 2,909 yards using a 112 ½ -lb bomb and a 2,976 ¼-lb iron gun carriage.

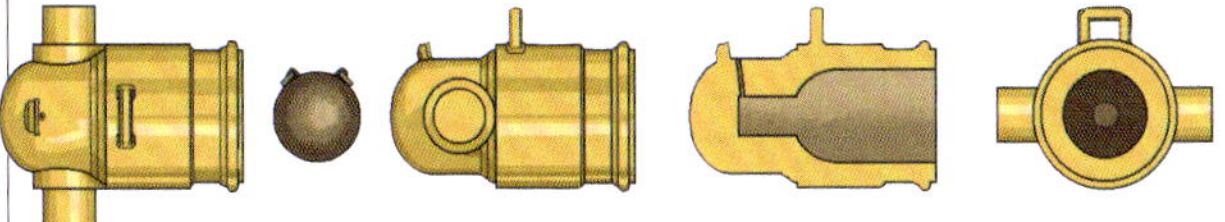

8-in, 21 ½ in long, cylindrical mortar weighing 639 ⅓ lbs with a maximum range of 1,203 yards using a 51-lb bomb and a 992-lb wooden gun carriage.

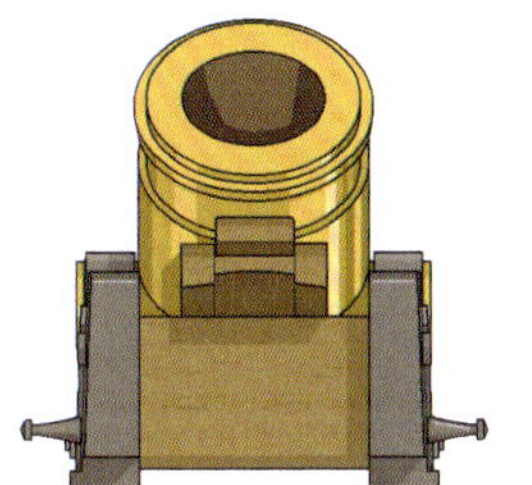

12-inch Mortar tilted at 45° on its gun carriage.

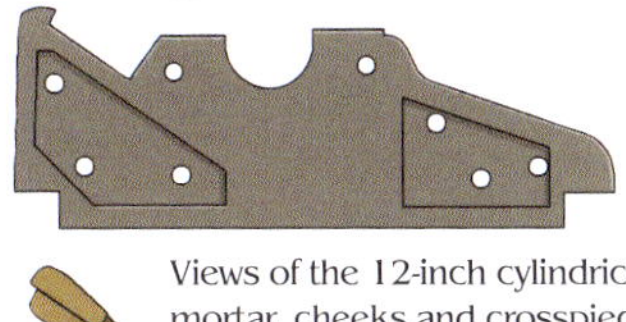

Views of the 12-inch cylindrical mortar, cheeks and crosspieces.

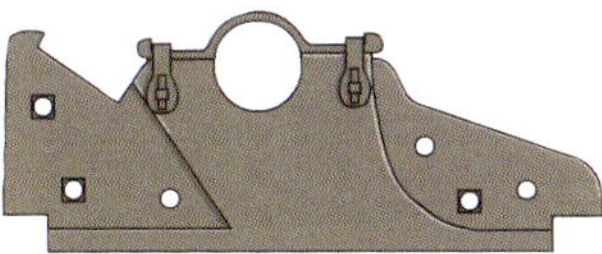

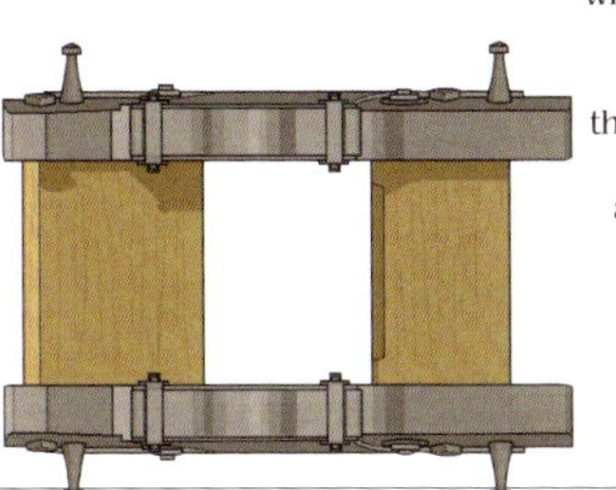

Serving the 12-inch cylindrical mortar on its platform. On the left there were two servants, the bombardier, two levers, two hooks for the 10- and 12-inch bombs, a swab, a rammer, a vent pricker, a bag of quick matches, a quarter circle, a double iron hook, a linstock 100 ft to the rear.

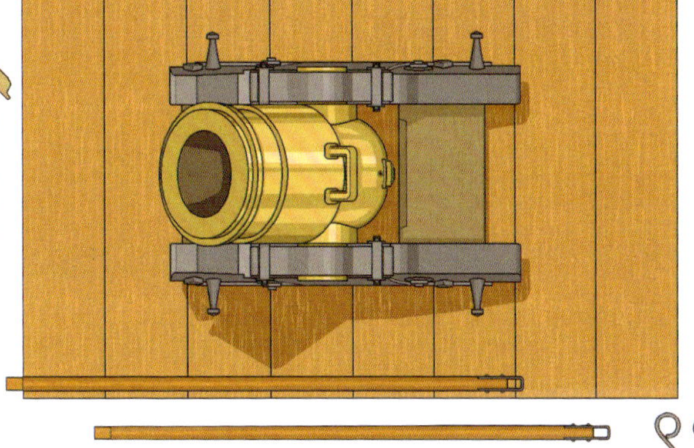

On the right were placed the two other servants with two levers, two aiming wedges, a broom and a basket containing the curette, a bag of earth, a plumb line, a spatula, a mallet, a *chasse fusée*, splints and pegs.

THE MORTAR WITH "A GOMER" TYPE FLAT CONE CHAMBER

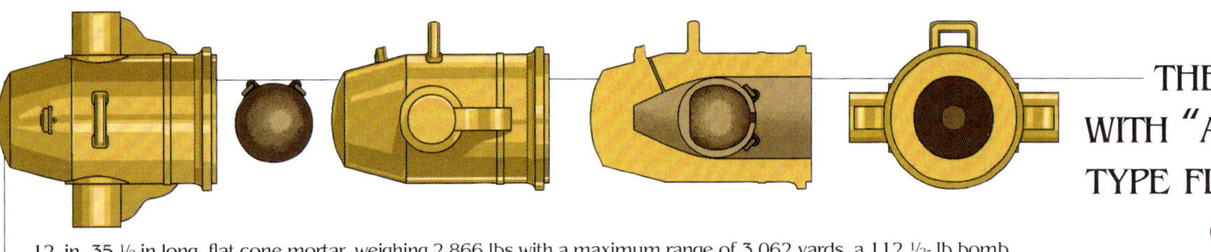
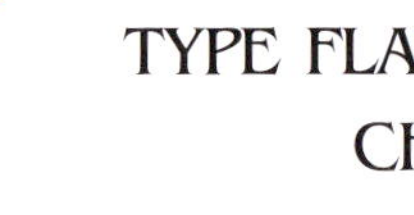

12- in, 35 ½-in long, flat cone mortar, weighing 2,866 lbs with a maximum range of 3,062 yards, a 112 ½- lb bomb and a 3,086 ½-lb iron gun carriage.

In 1785, the Chevalier de Gomer, *Maréchal de Camp* and Inspector of the Artillery Corps, perfected a new type of mortar with a flattened-cone shaped chamber. Put into service after 1791, the so-called "Gomer" mortar provided more thrust that the previous system since the projectile was wedged better inside the chamber.

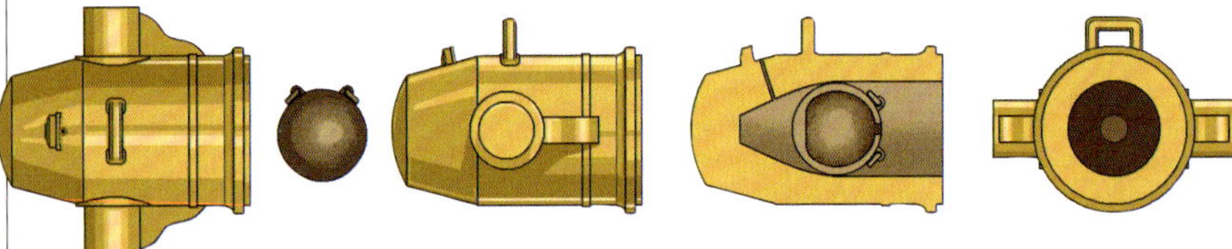

10-in, 29 ½-in long, flat cone mortar, weighing 2,050 $^{1}/_{3}$ lb with a maximum range of 3,062 yards, a 165 $^{1}/_{3}$-lb bomb and a 2,976 $^{1}/_{4}$-lb iron gun carriage.

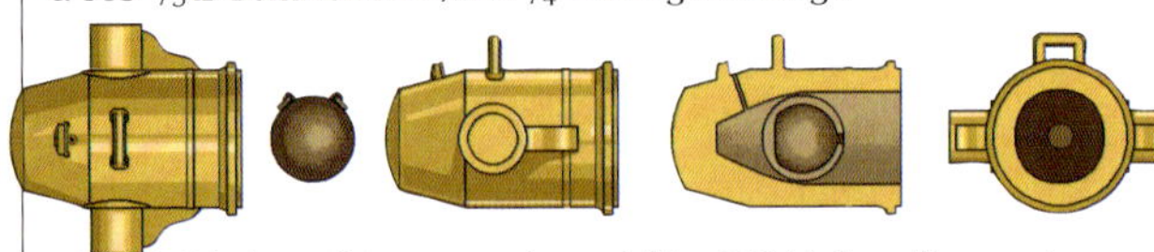

8-in, 21 ½-in long, flat cone mortar, weighing 639 $^{1}/_{3}$ lbs with a maximum range of 2,187 ¼ yards, a 50 ¾-lb bomb and a 992-lb wooden gun carriage.

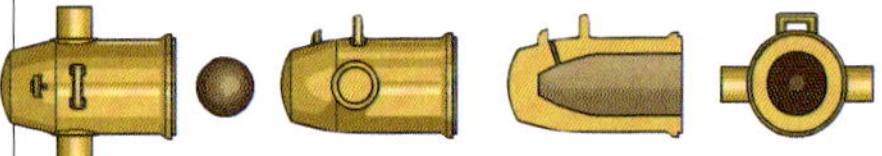

5 inch 7 line, 16 ½-in long, flat cone mortar, weighing 154 $^{1}/_{3}$ lbs with a maximum range of 656 yards, a 16 $^{1}/_{3}$-lb bomb and a 145 ½-lb wooden gun carriage.

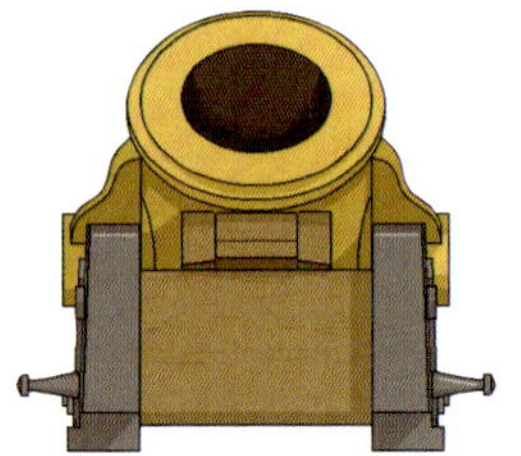

Front view and profile of a 12-inch mortar, tilted at 45°.

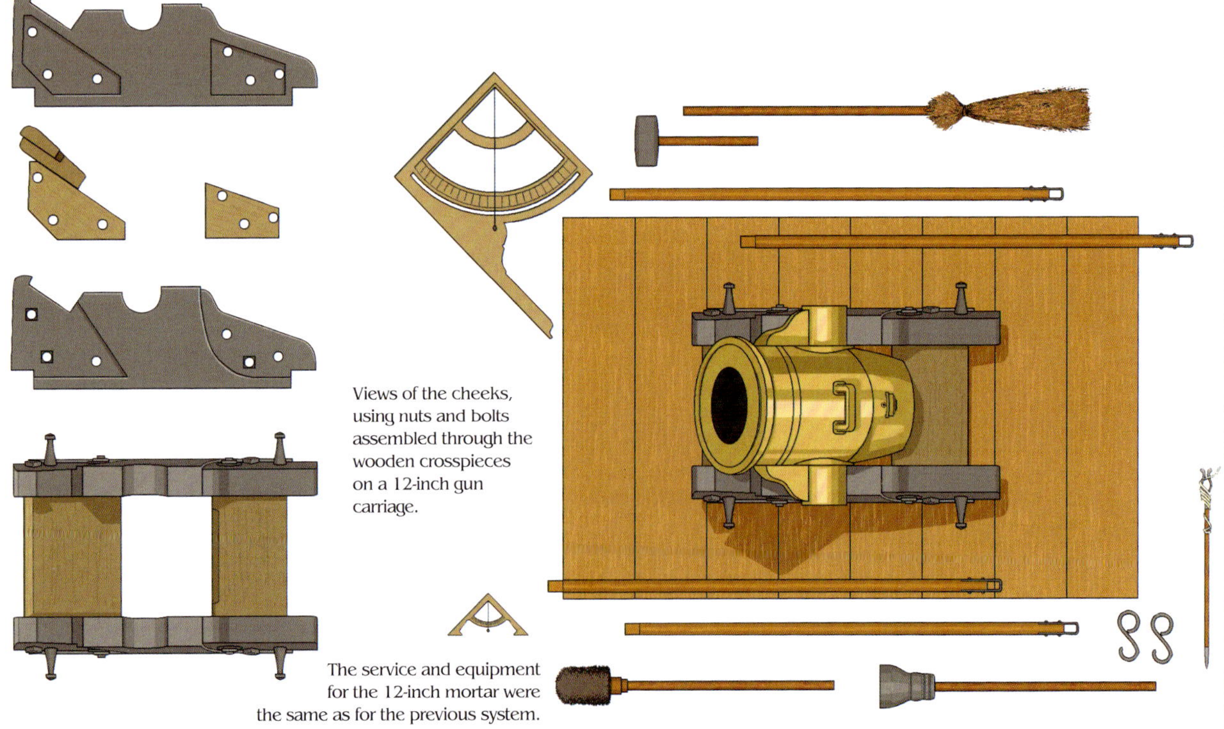

Views of the cheeks, using nuts and bolts assembled through the wooden crosspieces on a 12-inch gun carriage.

The service and equipment for the 12-inch mortar were the same as for the previous system.

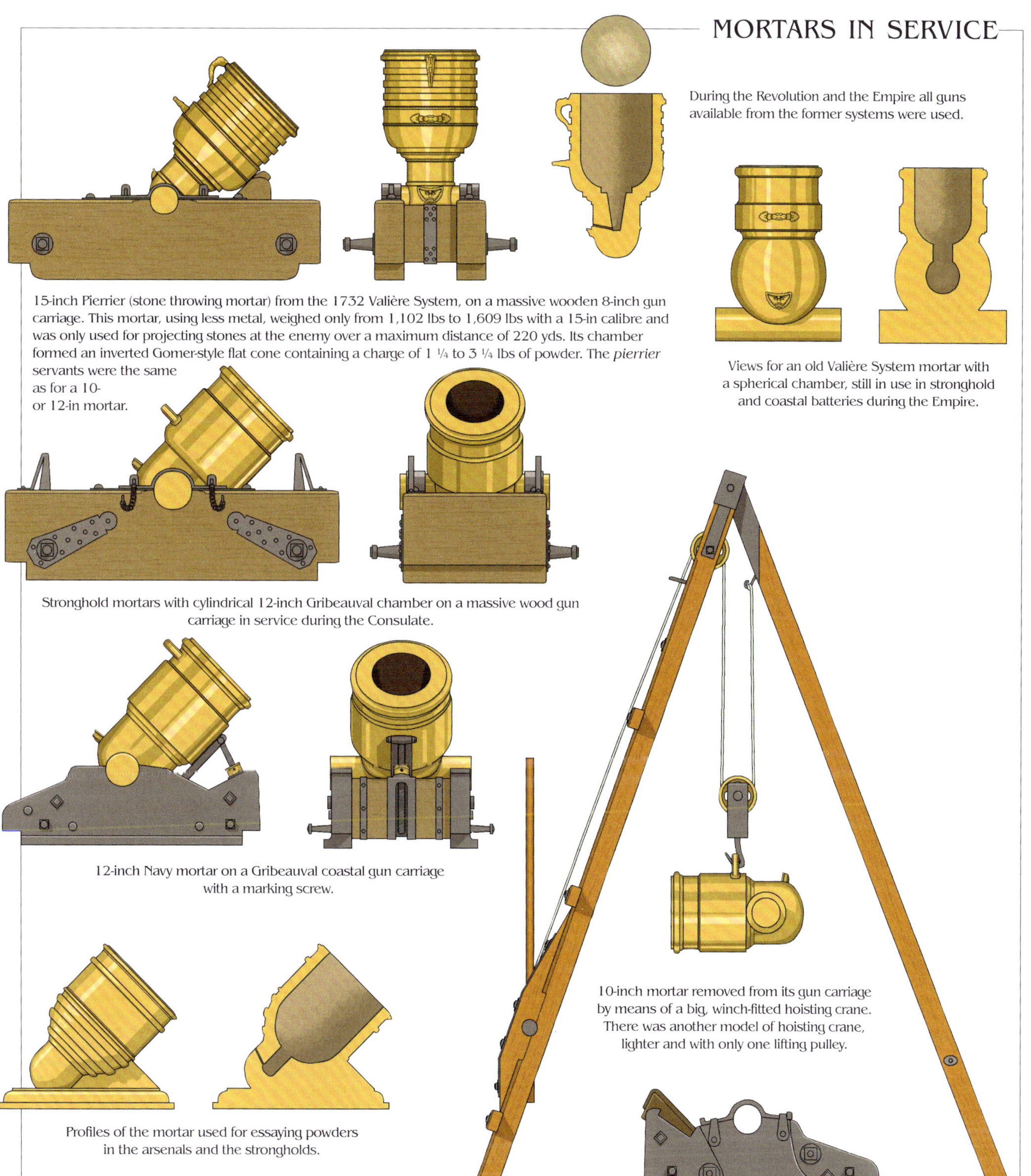

During the Revolution and the Empire all guns available from the former systems were used.

15-inch Pierrier (stone throwing mortar) from the 1732 Valière System, on a massive wooden 8-inch gun carriage. This mortar, using less metal, weighed only from 1,102 lbs to 1,609 lbs with a 15-in calibre and was only used for projecting stones at the enemy over a maximum distance of 220 yds. Its chamber formed an inverted Gomer-style flat cone containing a charge of 1 ¼ to 3 ¼ lbs of powder. The *pierrier* servants were the same as for a 10- or 12-in mortar.

Views for an old Valière System mortar with a spherical chamber, still in use in stronghold and coastal batteries during the Empire.

Stronghold mortars with cylindrical 12-inch Gribeauval chamber on a massive wood gun carriage in service during the Consulate.

12-inch Navy mortar on a Gribeauval coastal gun carriage with a marking screw.

10-inch mortar removed from its gun carriage by means of a big, winch-fitted hoisting crane. There was another model of hoisting crane, lighter and with only one lifting pulley.

Profiles of the mortar used for essaying powders in the arsenals and the strongholds.

SERVING THE MORTAR

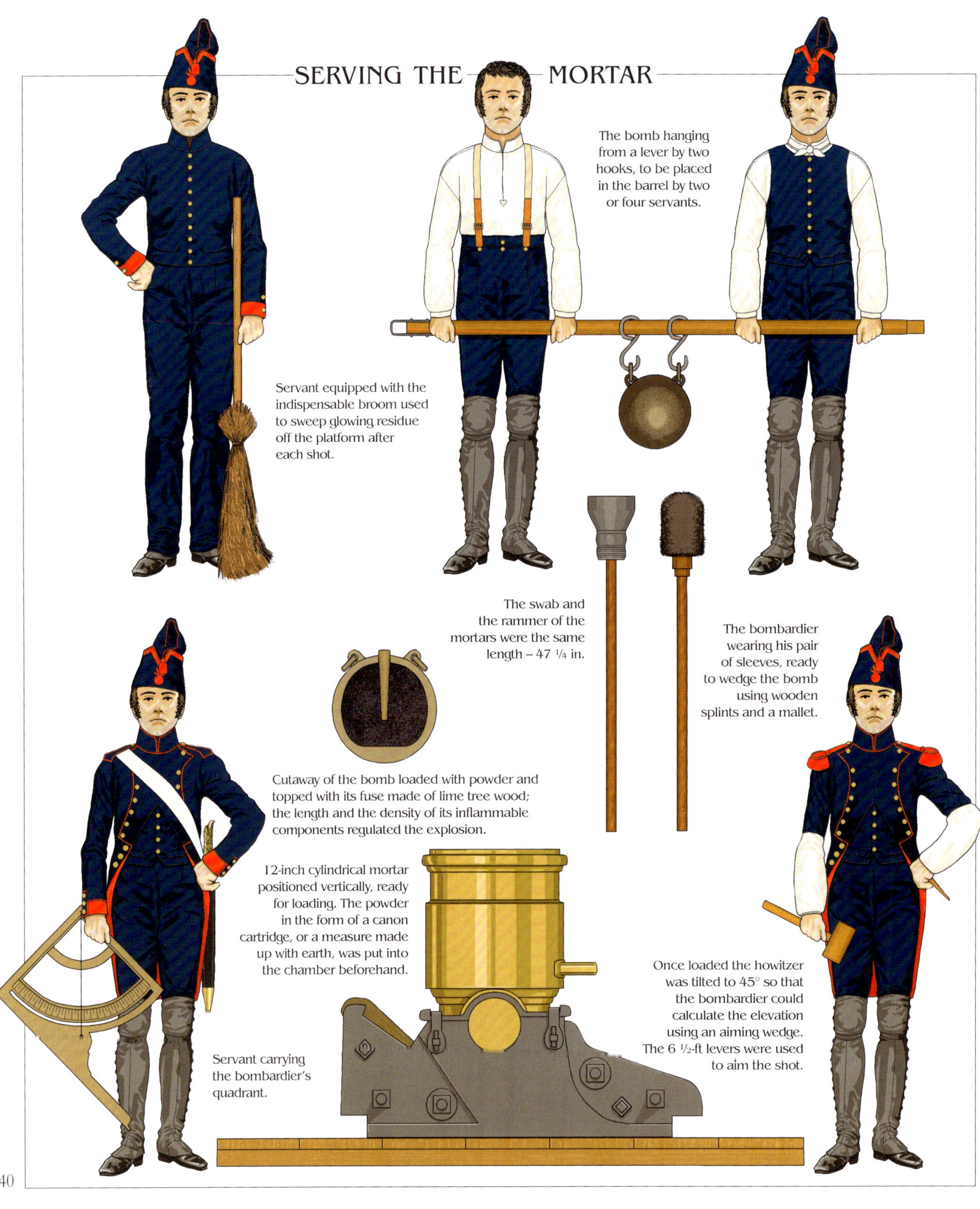

THE MORTAR ON A SLEEPER FROM AN XI

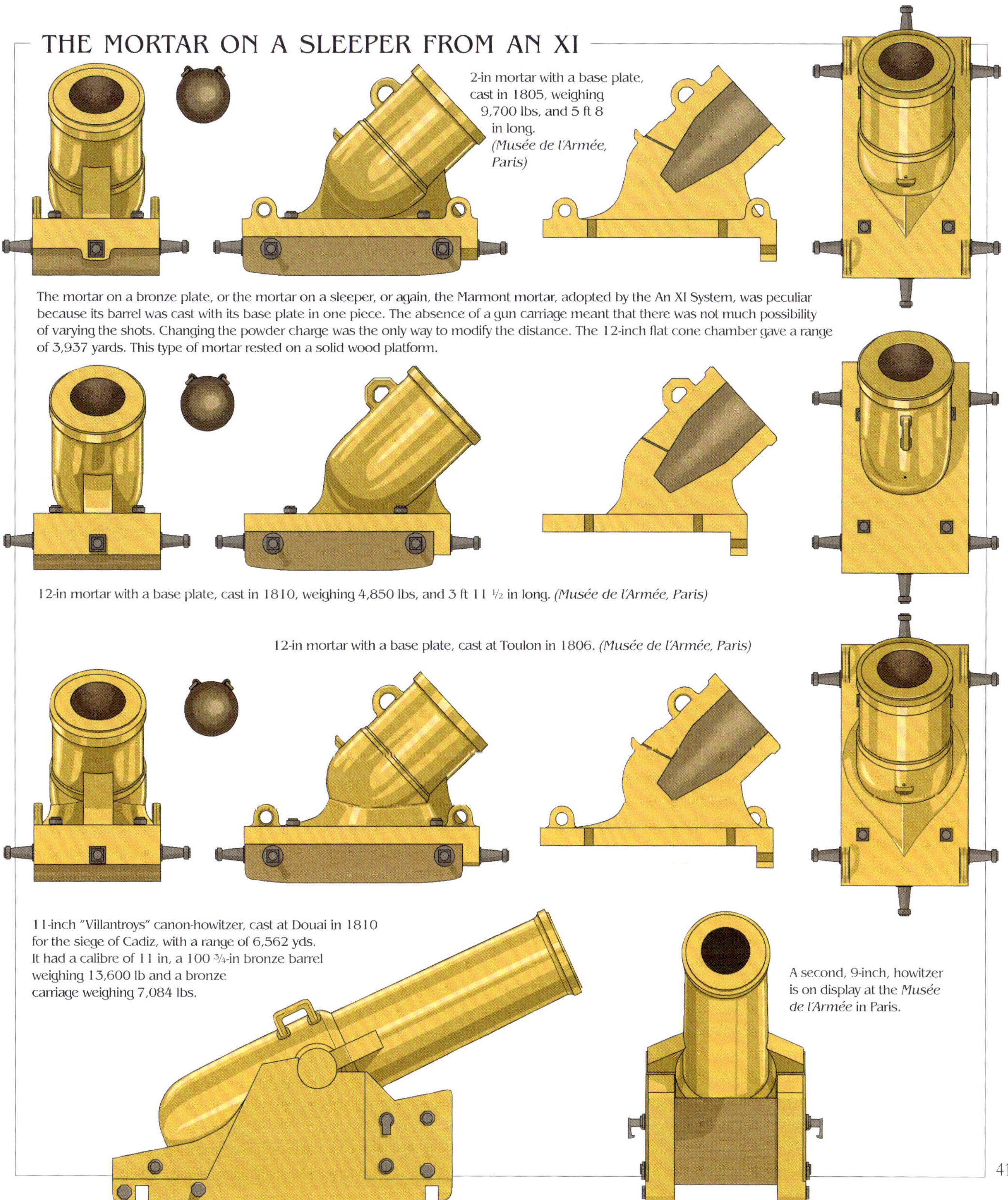

2-in mortar with a base plate, cast in 1805, weighing 9,700 lbs, and 5 ft 8 in long. *(Musée de l'Armée, Paris)*

The mortar on a bronze plate, or the mortar on a sleeper, or again, the Marmont mortar, adopted by the An XI System, was peculiar because its barrel was cast with its base plate in one piece. The absence of a gun carriage meant that there was not much possibility of varying the shots. Changing the powder charge was the only way to modify the distance. The 12-inch flat cone chamber gave a range of 3,937 yards. This type of mortar rested on a solid wood platform.

12-in mortar with a base plate, cast in 1810, weighing 4,850 lbs, and 3 ft 11 ½ in long. *(Musée de l'Armée, Paris)*

12-in mortar with a base plate, cast at Toulon in 1806. *(Musée de l'Armée, Paris)*

11-inch "Villantroys" canon-howitzer, cast at Douai in 1810 for the siege of Cadiz, with a range of 6,562 yds. It had a calibre of 11 in, a 100 ¾-in bronze barrel weighing 13,600 lb and a bronze carriage weighing 7,084 lbs.

A second, 9-inch, howitzer is on display at the *Musée de l'Armée* in Paris.

THE GRIBEAUVAL 8-, 12- AND 16-LB STRONGHOLD GUN CARRIAGES

- 8-lb canon on a 6-ft long Gribeauval stronghold carriage, with 37 1/2 in high cheeks, a 12-ft chassis and a 6-ft platform.

12-lb canon on Gribeauval stronghold carriage, with 6 1/2-ft long and 37-inch high cheeks, a 12-ft chassis and a platform 5 ft 10 long.

16-lb canon on 7-ft long Gribeauval stronghold carriage, with 37 1/2-in high cheeks, a 12-ft chassis and a platform 6 1/2 ft long.
The gap between the cheeks, and the grooves on the chassis were the same for the four calibres.
The 16- and 24-lb stronghold gun barrels were shorter than the siege barrels.

THE GRIBEAUVAL 24-LB STRONGHOLD GUN CARRIAGE

The Gribeauval System set up new batteries in the strongholds comprising 8-, 12-, 16- and 24-lb guns. They were modelled on naval gun carriages to enable five servants, including two bombardiers, to fire through the embrasures along the parapets and to reload quite safely.

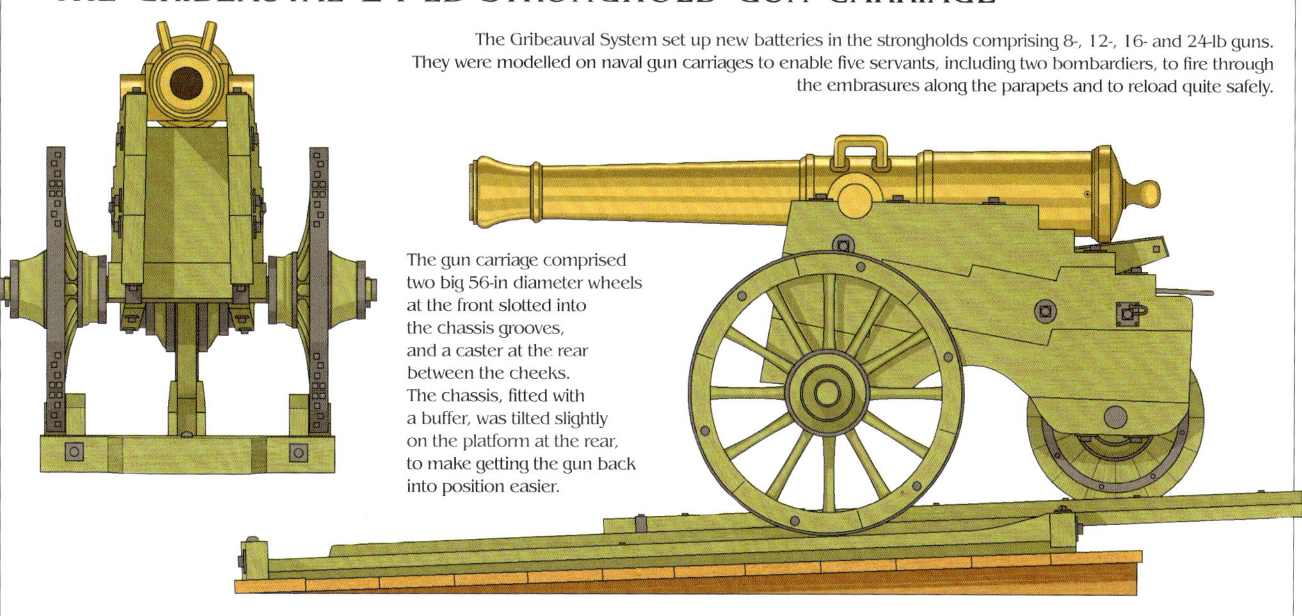

The gun carriage comprised two big 56-in diameter wheels at the front slotted into the chassis grooves, and a caster at the rear between the cheeks. The chassis, fitted with a buffer, was tilted slightly on the platform at the rear, to make getting the gun back into position easier.

A king bolt stuck on the front of the chassis enabled the gun to swivel sideways.

The complete equipment for a gun comprised a cap, a broom, four levers, two stop wedges, a vent pricker, a bag of quick matches, a percussion cap, two aiming wedges, a swab with a rammer, a lantern and a gun wadding puller, cannonballs and stoppers.

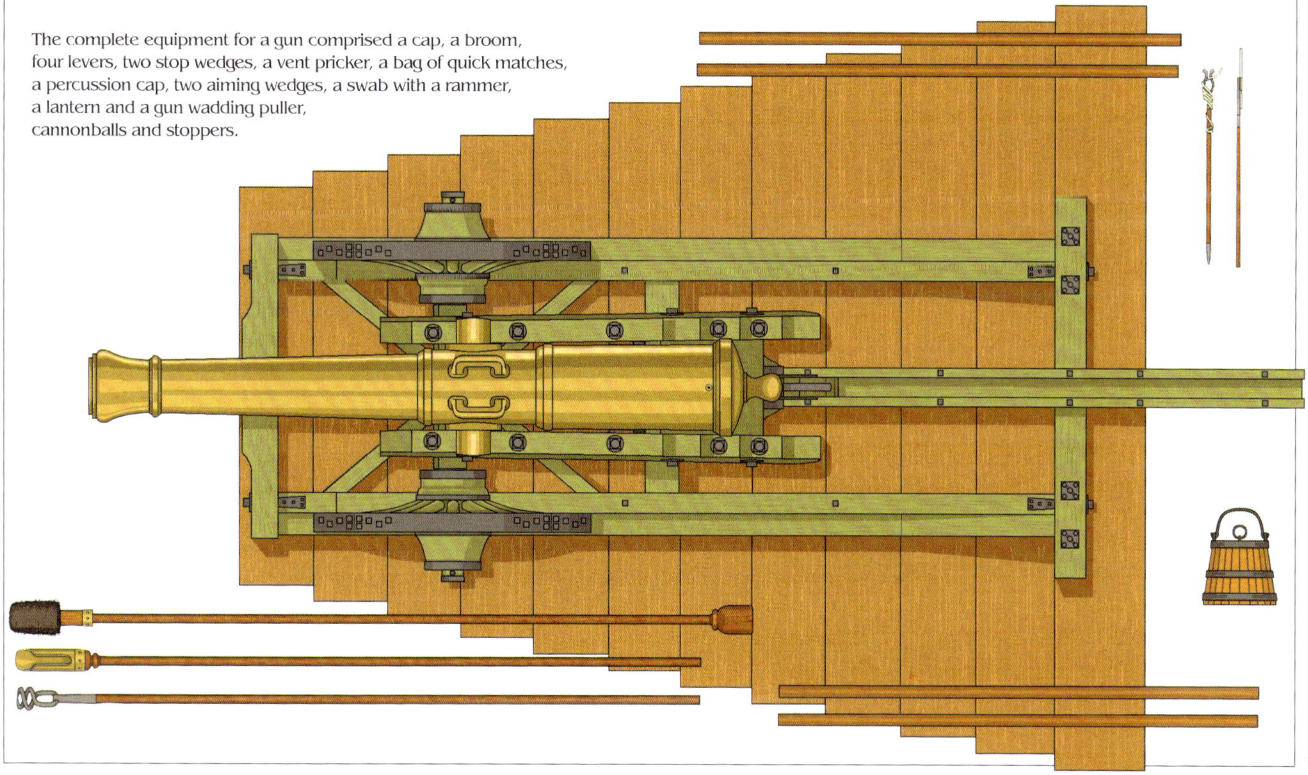

THE NEW 8 12 AND 16-LB STRONGHOLD GUN CARRIAGES

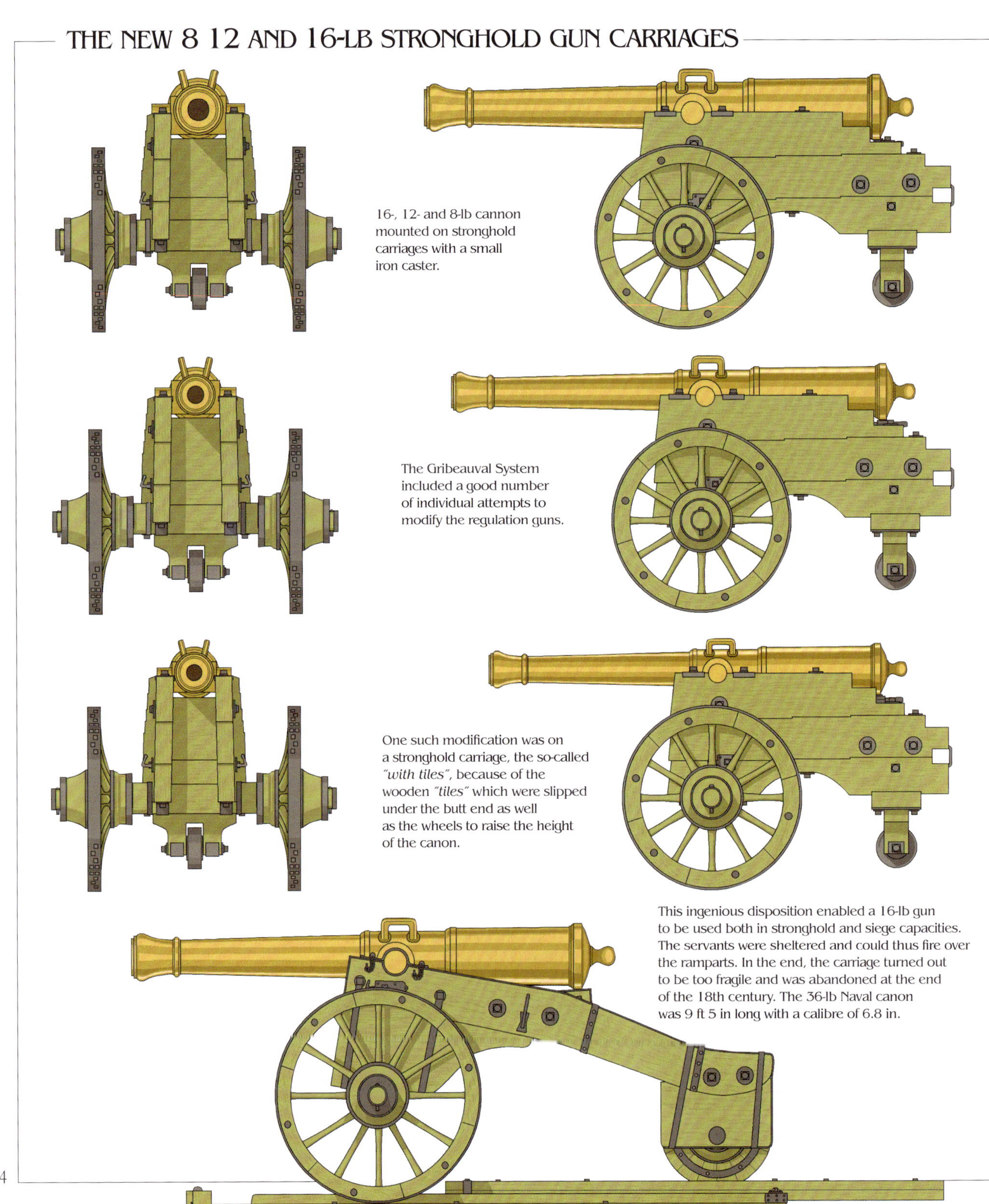

16-, 12- and 8-lb cannon mounted on stronghold carriages with a small iron caster.

The Gribeauval System included a good number of individual attempts to modify the regulation guns.

One such modification was on a stronghold carriage, the so-called *"with tiles"*, because of the wooden *"tiles"* which were slipped under the butt end as well as the wheels to raise the height of the canon.

This ingenious disposition enabled a 16-lb gun to be used both in stronghold and siege capacities. The servants were sheltered and could thus fire over the ramparts. In the end, the carriage turned out to be too fragile and was abandoned at the end of the 18th century. The 36-lb Naval canon was 9 ft 5 in long with a calibre of 6.8 in.

THE NEW 24-LB STRONGHOLD GUN CARRIAGE

The An-XI System recommended lighter and shorter 6-, 12- and 24-lb guns for siege and stronghold artillery. These new barrels were unsuitable for use as such and had to be fitted with a muzzle brake in order to suppress the flame back outside the fortification embrasures. This type of canon does not appear to have been cast.

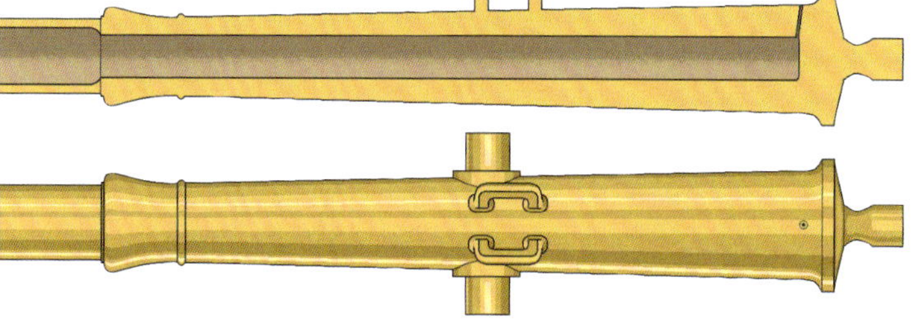

24-lb stronghold carriage, using the same construction principles as the Gribeauval model but with a smaller iron caster. The lower centre of gravity on this model made the gun carriage more stable on the chassis.

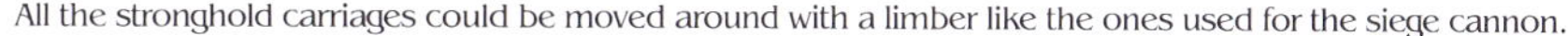

All the stronghold carriages could be moved around with a limber like the ones used for the siege cannon.

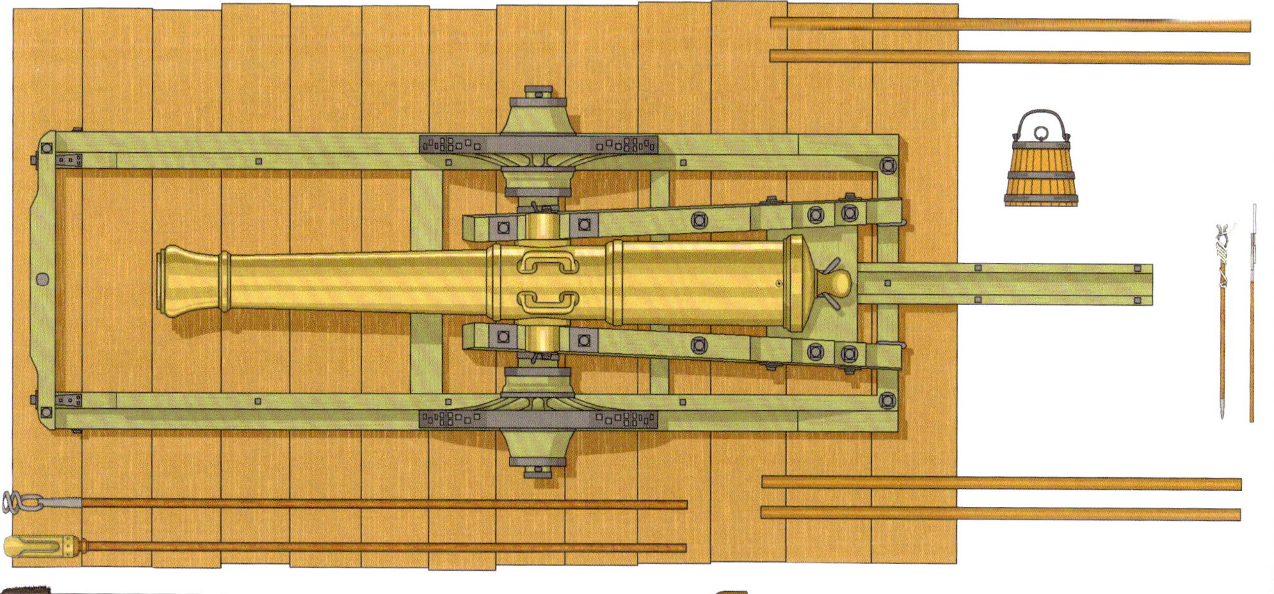

CANONNIERS SÉDENTAIRES DE LILLE 1789-1809

Lille Permanent Gunner in 1789 wearing summer dress.

Officer in the *Canonniers Sédentaires de Lille* (the Lille Permanent Gunners) during the Revolution, after the portrait of Captain Charlemagne Ovigneur.

Lille Permanent Gunner wearing full dress towards 1803-1806. The uniform is that of the Foot Artillery with a blue collar without piping, Hussar-style boots edged with red and a hat decorated with aurora braid and a red and dark blue plume.

Lille Permanent Gunner towards 1811-1812, wearing ordinary uniform as shown by the red pompom.

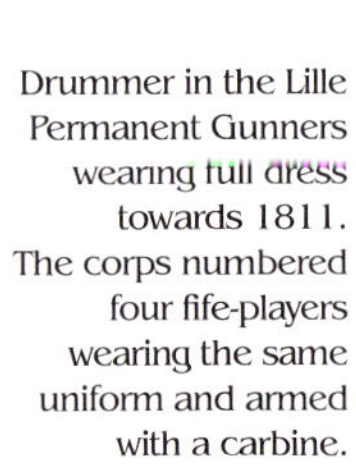

Drummer in the Lille Permanent Gunners wearing full dress towards 1811. The corps numbered four fife-players wearing the same uniform and armed with a carbine.

Corporal in the Lille Permanent Gunners wearing full dress towards 1806-1811.

Flag presented on 8 December 1812 to the Lille Permanent Gunners. The obverse bore the inscription MURORUM INVICTA DEFENSIO with the date 2 MAI 1483. The reverse side bore the inscription CORPS IMPERIAL DES CANONNIERS SEDENTAIRES DE LILLE.
The blue pole was surmounted by a copper point.

812-model artillery shako plate with two crossed cannon and CANONNIERS DE LILLE on the escutcheon.

Lille Permanent Gunners pompoms

Uniform button stamped with a flaming bomb and the inscription CANONNIERS DE LILLE CREES EN 1483.

Lille Permanent sapper wearing full dress in 1811. In ordinary dress the sapper wore a plateless shako.

Drummer in the Lille Permanent Gunners during the Hundred Days, wearing a blue coat of the former Royal livery decorated with the Imperial braid.

Lille Permanent Gunner towards 1813-1815.

Officer in the Lille Permanent Artillery in 1813. The shako was edged with black velvet braid and surmounted with a white plume and the headquarters lentil.

THE CHERBOURG SWIVEL PIN GUN CARRIAGE

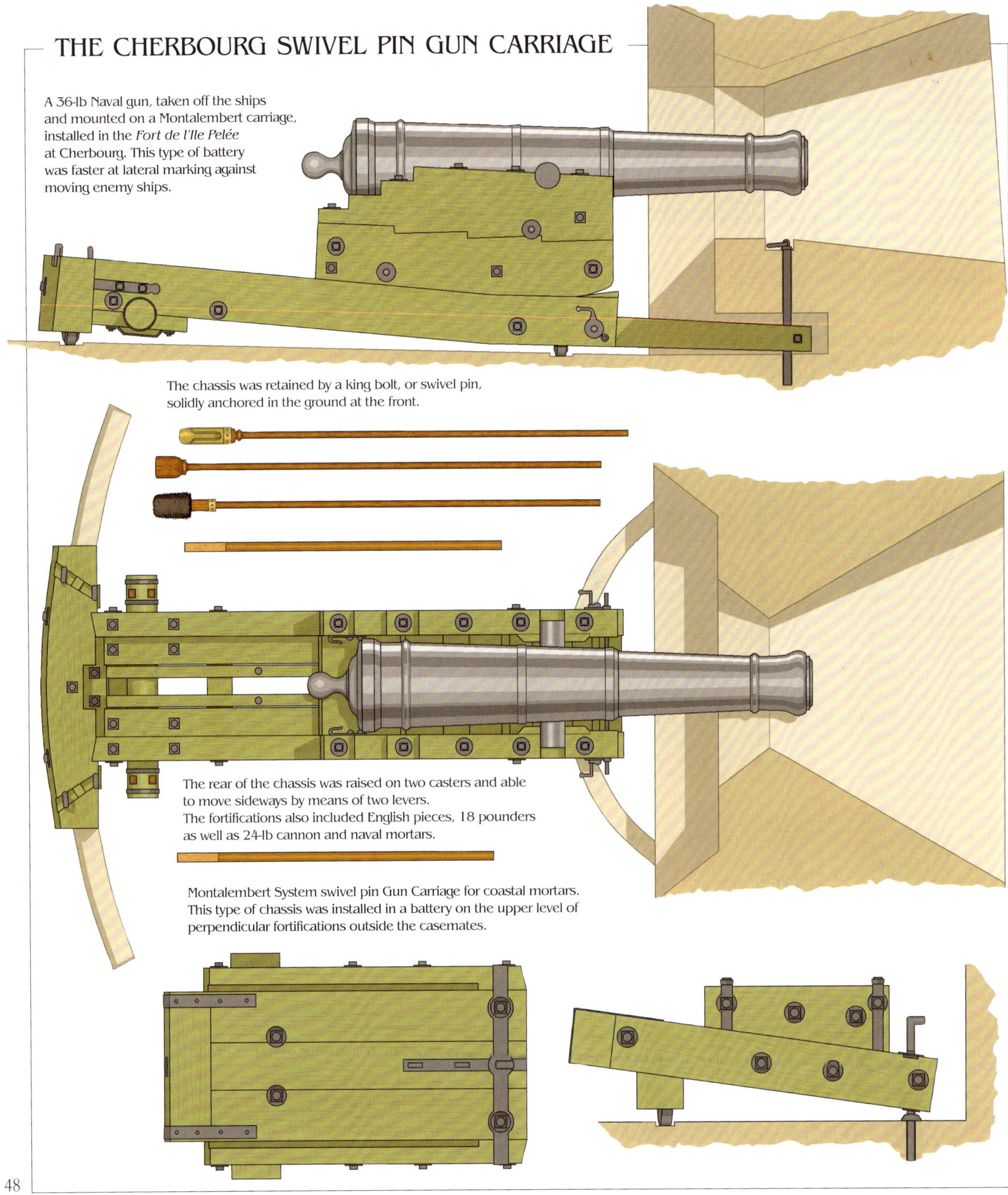

A 36-lb Naval gun, taken off the ships and mounted on a Montalembert carriage, installed in the *Fort de l'Ile Pelée* at Cherbourg. This type of battery was faster at lateral marking against moving enemy ships.

The chassis was retained by a king bolt, or swivel pin, solidly anchored in the ground at the front.

The rear of the chassis was raised on two casters and able to move sideways by means of two levers.
The fortifications also included English pieces, 18 pounders as well as 24-lb cannon and naval mortars.

Montalembert System swivel pin Gun Carriage for coastal mortars. This type of chassis was installed in a battery on the upper level of perpendicular fortifications outside the casemates.

THE AIX SWIVEL PIN GUN CARRIAGE

A Naval cast iron 6.8 in calibre 36-lb gun, 9 ft 5 in long on a carriage and a chassis using a swivel pin. This gun was part of the battery set up inside the *Fort de la Sommité* on the Isle of Aix in 1779. The fort was destroyed in 1810; it had 180 guns on swivel pin carriages inside the casemates. This type of chassis inside a casemate was designed by the Marquis de Montalembert for the coastal bastions to replace the old Gribeauval System batteries. It meant building new types of fortifications, the so-called "perpendicular" type, enabling the servants to shelter in casemates which were open at the rear only to get rid of the smoke.

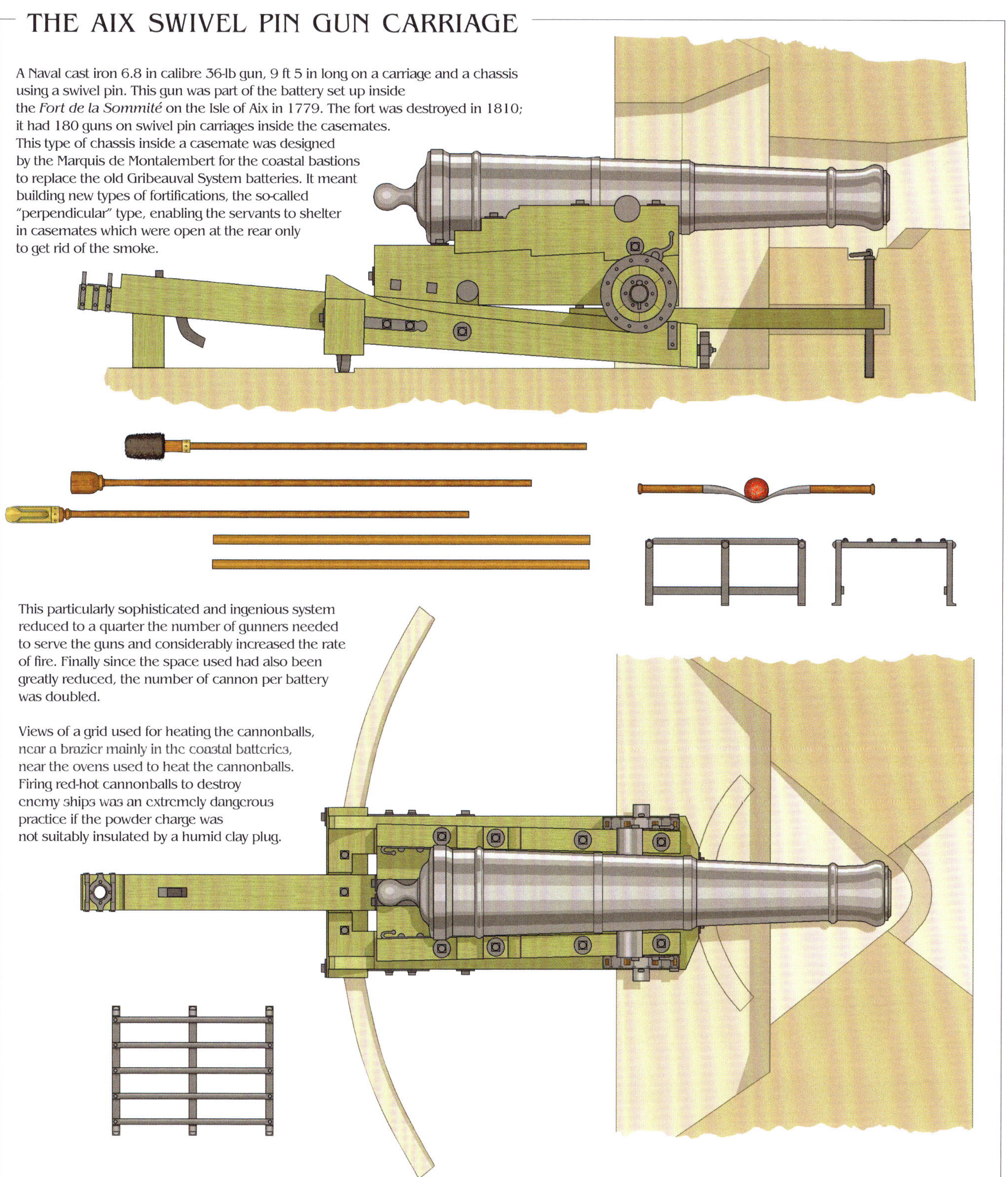

This particularly sophisticated and ingenious system reduced to a quarter the number of gunners needed to serve the guns and considerably increased the rate of fire. Finally since the space used had also been greatly reduced, the number of cannon per battery was doubled.

Views of a grid used for heating the cannonballs, near a brazier mainly in the coastal batteries, near the ovens used to heat the cannonballs. Firing red-hot cannonballs to destroy enemy ships was an extremely dangerous practice if the powder charge was not suitably insulated by a humid clay plug.

THE 12-LB NAVAL CANON ON A COASTAL GUN CARRIAGE

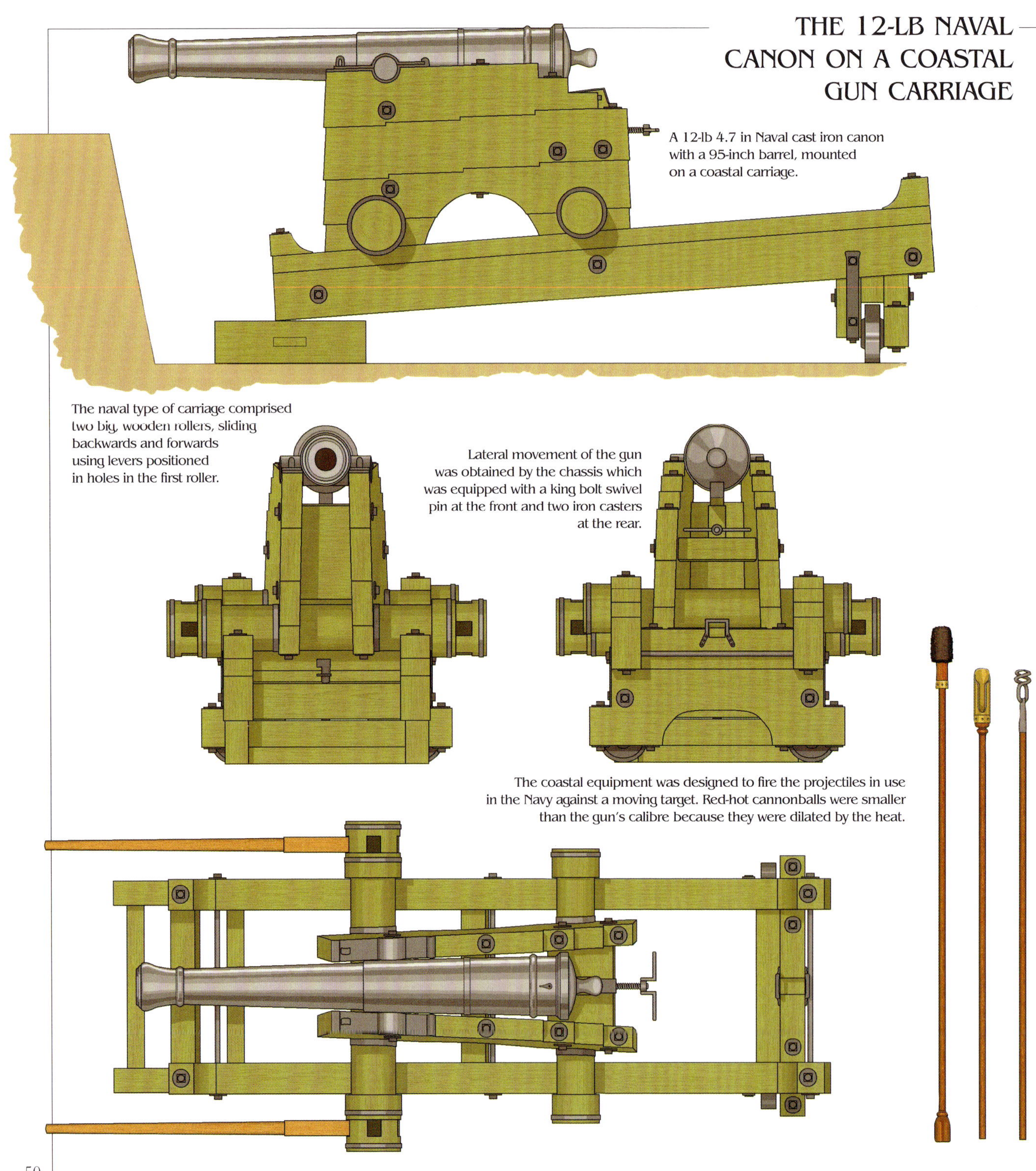

A 12-lb 4.7 in Naval cast iron canon with a 95-inch barrel, mounted on a coastal carriage.

The naval type of carriage comprised two big, wooden rollers, sliding backwards and forwards using levers positioned in holes in the first roller.

Lateral movement of the gun was obtained by the chassis which was equipped with a king bolt swivel pin at the front and two iron casters at the rear.

The coastal equipment was designed to fire the projectiles in use in the Navy against a moving target. Red-hot cannonballs were smaller than the gun's calibre because they were dilated by the heat.

THE 16-LB NAVAL CANON ON A COASTAL GUN CARRIAGE

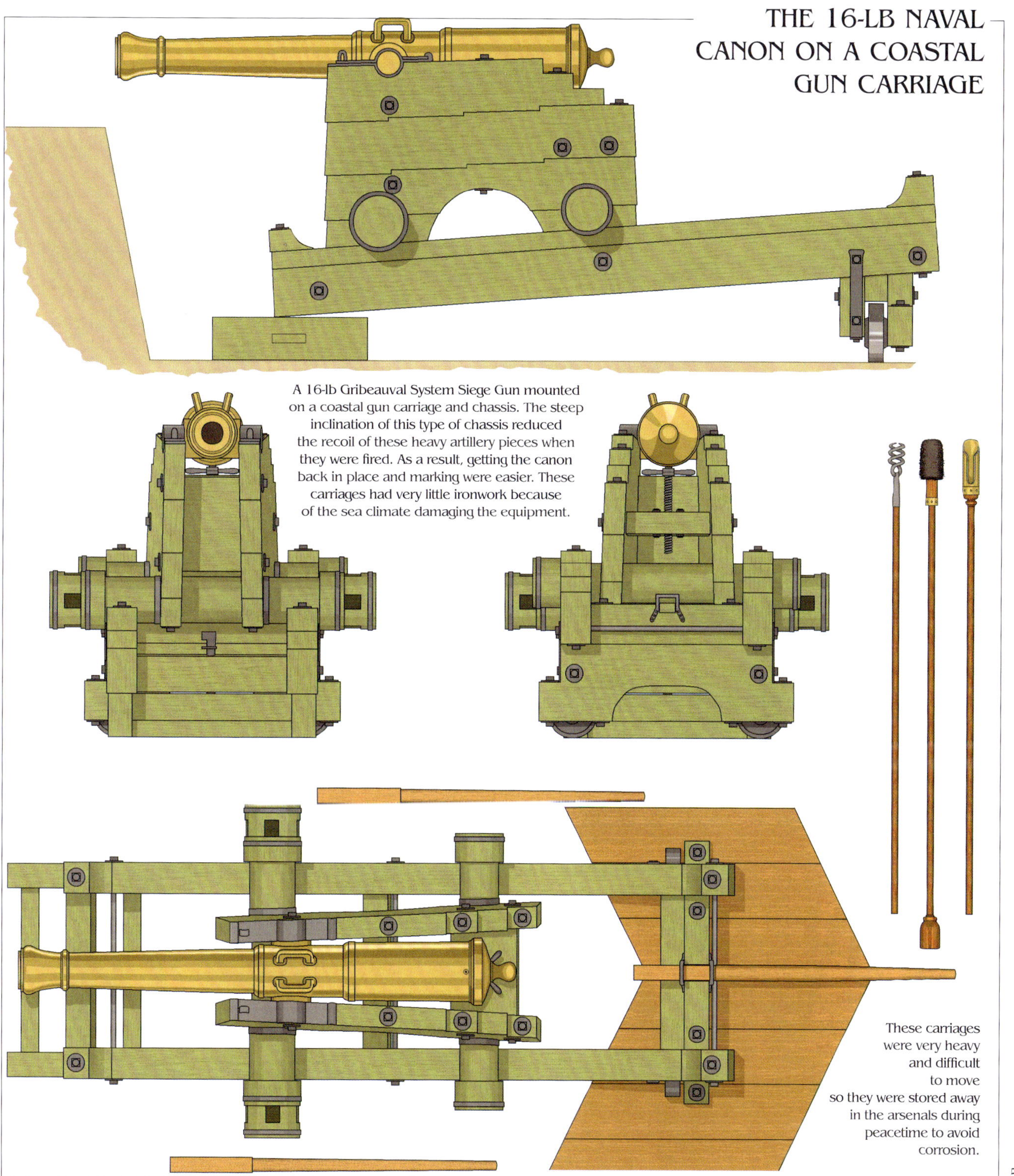

A 16-lb Gribeauval System Siege Gun mounted on a coastal gun carriage and chassis. The steep inclination of this type of chassis reduced the recoil of these heavy artillery pieces when they were fired. As a result, getting the canon back in place and marking were easier. These carriages had very little ironwork because of the sea climate damaging the equipment.

These carriages were very heavy and difficult to move so they were stored away in the arsenals during peacetime to avoid corrosion.

THE 24-LB NAVAL CANON ON A COASTAL GUN CARRIAGE

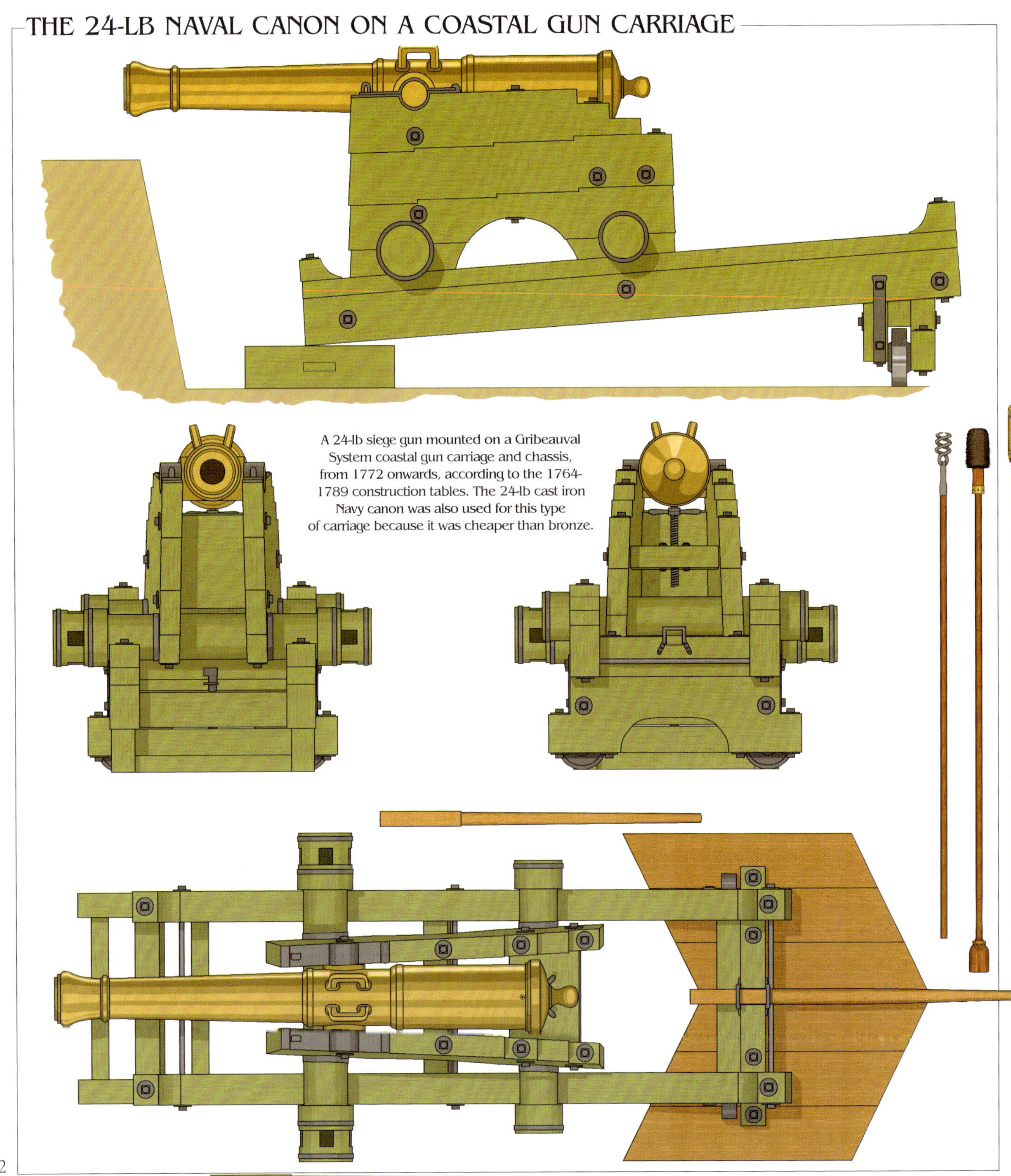

A 24-lb siege gun mounted on a Gribeauval System coastal gun carriage and chassis, from 1772 onwards, according to the 1764-1789 construction tables. The 24-lb cast iron Navy canon was also used for this type of carriage because it was cheaper than bronze.

THE 18-LB NAVAL CANON ON THE OLDER COASTAL GUN CARRIAGE

An 18-lb 5.4 in calibre cast iron Navy gun with an 8 ft long barrel. The Navy type carriage rested on four big wooden wheels and could move backwards and forwards.
The tilted chassis could move sideways on the front swivel bolt and a fifth big wooden wheel at the rear. All the *chasses* rested on wooden platforms.

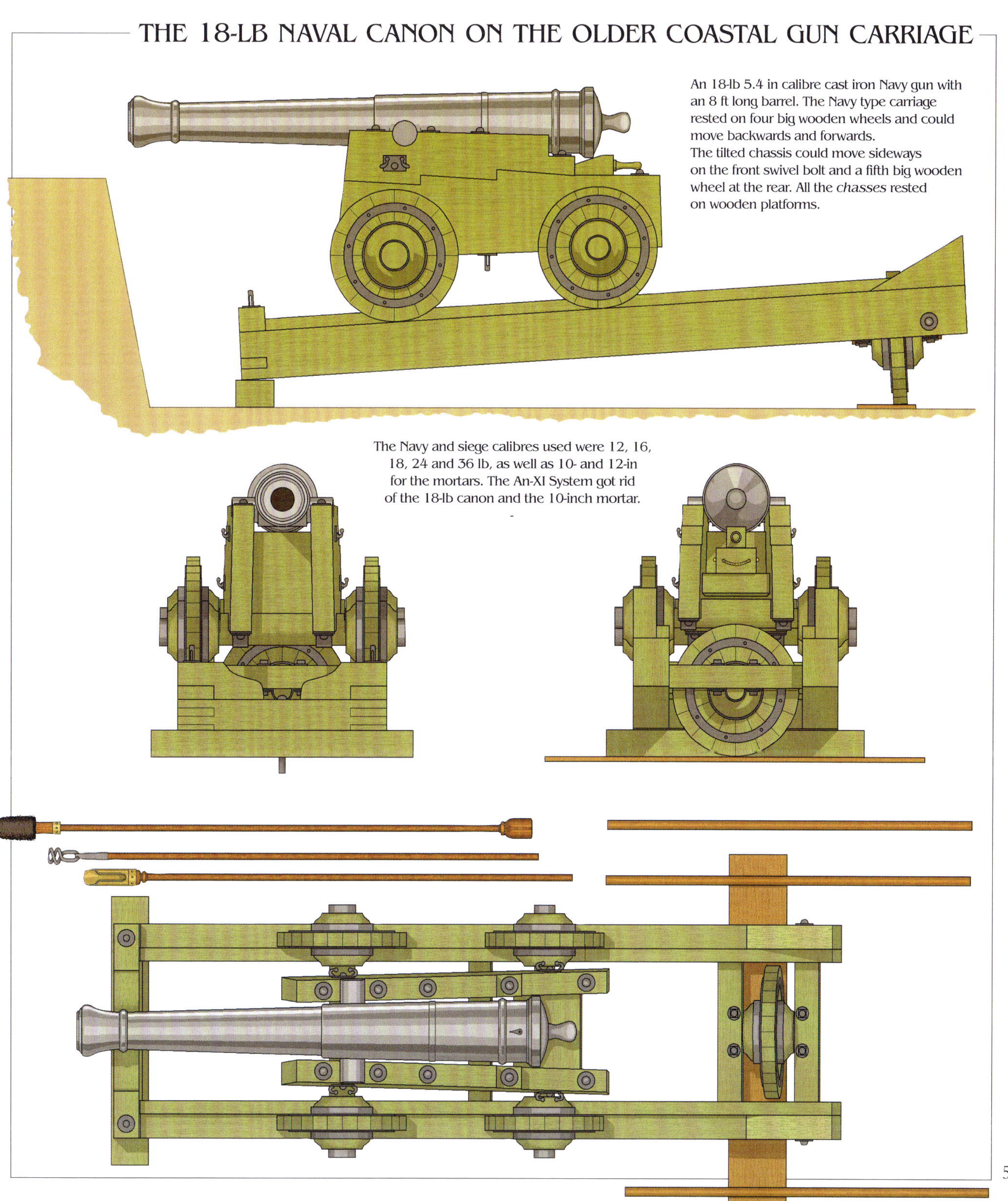

The Navy and siege calibres used were 12, 16, 18, 24 and 36 lb, as well as 10- and 12-in for the mortars. The An-XI System got rid of the 18-lb canon and the 10-inch mortar.

THE 24-LB NAVAL CANON ON THE OLDER COASTAL GUN CARRIAGE

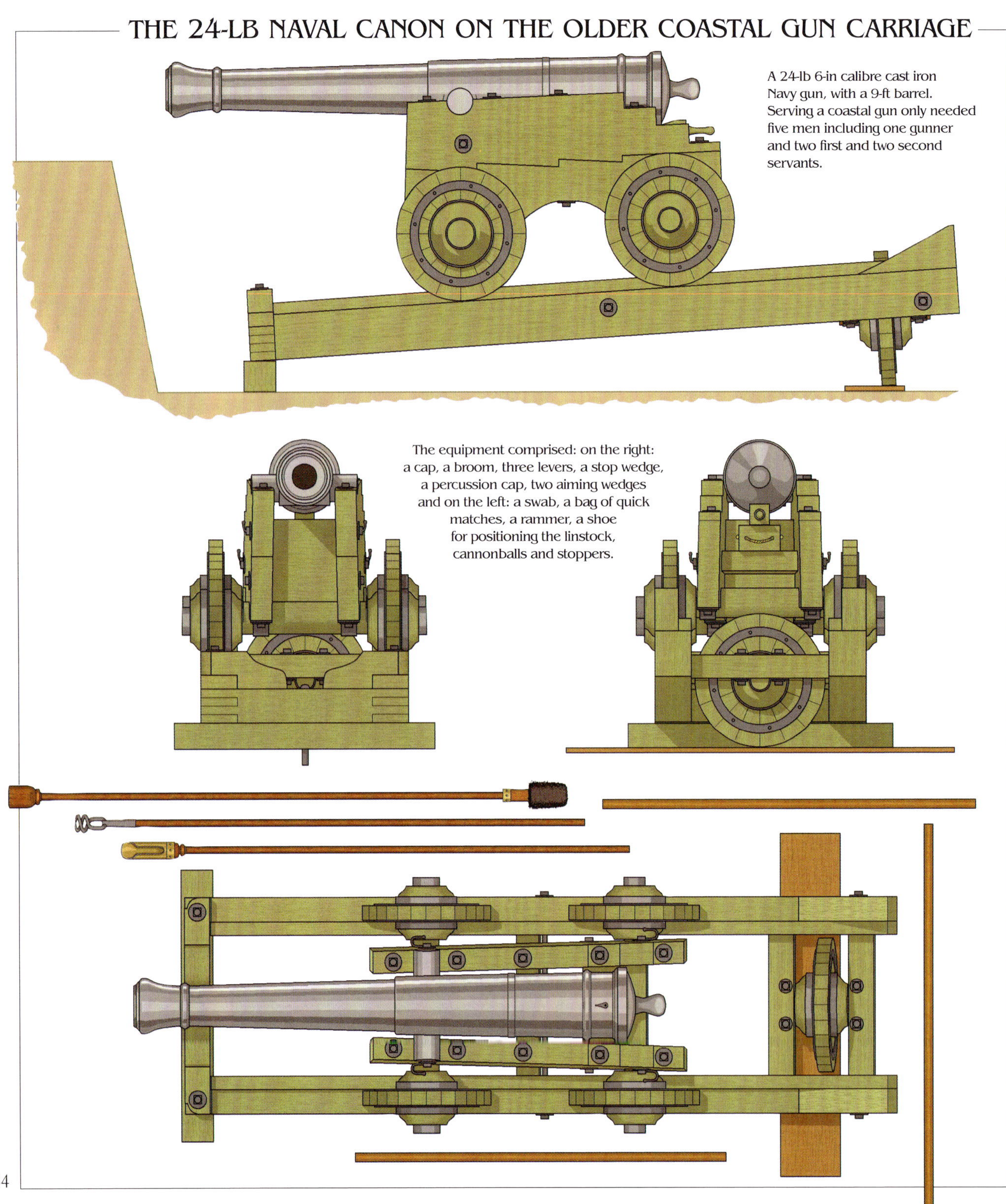

A 24-lb 6-in calibre cast iron Navy gun, with a 9-ft barrel. Serving a coastal gun only needed five men including one gunner and two first and two second servants.

The equipment comprised: on the right: a cap, a broom, three levers, a stop wedge, a percussion cap, two aiming wedges and on the left: a swab, a bag of quick matches, a rammer, a shoe for positioning the linstock, cannonballs and stoppers.

COASTGUARD GUNNERS 1794-1803

The 1786-model copper button was stamped with a canon over a crossed anchor and rifle.

Coastguard gunners and officers in 1794 wearing a dark blue coat distinguished with sea green on the collar, the lapels, the facing flaps, the grenades on the turnbacks and on the edging of the shoulder flaps and the slanted pockets.

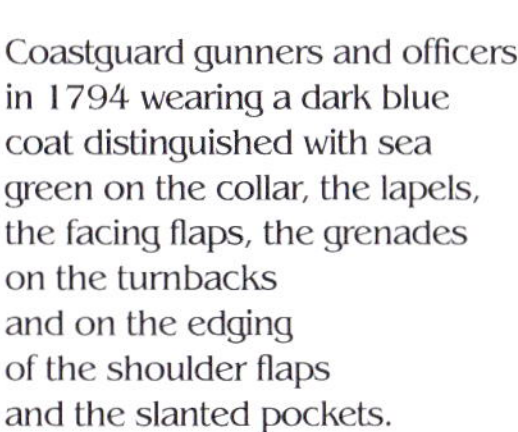

The breeches and waistcoat were sea green.

Coastguard officer, gunner and drummer wearing full dress from 1803 to 1807. The coat had pockets lengthwise and white turnbacks decorated with blue grenades.

The uniform button bore a crossed rifle and canon in front of an anchor.

The shoulder flaps were replaced by red epaulets.

The hat was decorated with aurora cord and a pompom the same colour as the company.

The weapons were those of the infantry.

COASTGUARD GUNNERS – 1807-1810

Coastguard gunners in around 1807-1810, according to Valmont. The uniform was entirely white with blue lapels, collar, facings and flaps, lining and slanted pocket edging. The grenades on the turnbacks were white and the greatcoat grey.

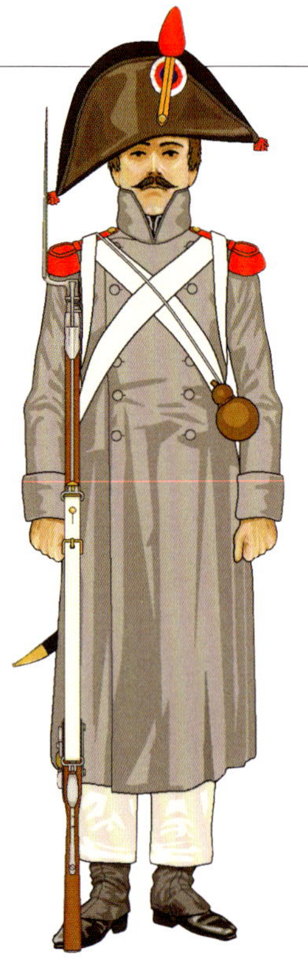

Gunner wearing drill dress with a white jacket and blue forage cap with scarlet piping.

Officers towards 1807-1810, after Valmont. The uniform was identical to that of the common soldiers except for the white turnbacks, red facing flaps and blue greatcoat.

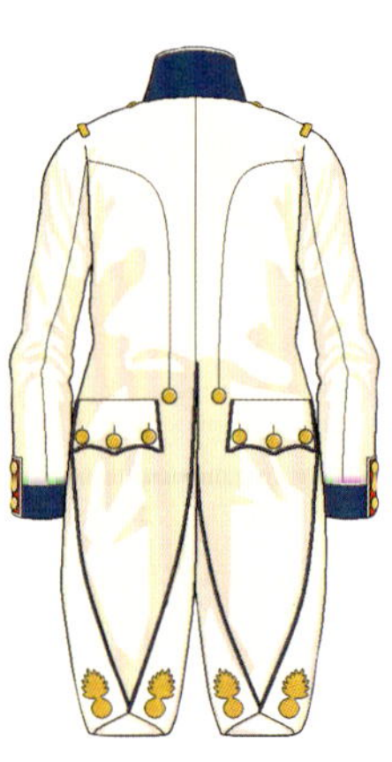

COASTGUARD GUNNERS 1810-1813

The shako had a cut-out plate with the same motif as the ornament on the cartridge box.

The documents show us quite a variety of details for the 1810-1813 period, like on this officer's uniform which was once again made of dark blue cloth distinguished with sea green and edged with white.

Variant of the uniform of a coastguard gunner in 1810, with scarlet edging on the coat.

Appointee wearing service dress towards 1810-1813. *(Reconstitution)*

Coastguard gunner, front and rear views, wearing the uniform conforming to the regulations from 1810 onwards.

COAST GUARDS GUNNERS 1810-1815

Corporal wearing full dress towards 1810-1813 with a coat entirely distinguished with sea green, and a blue greatcoat.

Variant of the uniform worn in about 1810-1813, with the coat piped with scarlet, the turnbacks and the pocket borders edged with white, as well as dark blue waistcoat and breeches.

Cartridge pouches for the coastguards with both models of plates used during the Empire.

Coastguard drummer in 1812, with a dark blue coat edged in the Imperial livery.

Coastguard gunner in 1814, according to the Bardin Regulations

1812-model copper Coastguard gunner's shako plate.

Coastguard gunner wearing a greatcoat towards 1810-1814.

1806 and 1812-model shako plates, attributed numberless to the companies of the Permanent Gunners.

Soldier from an ordinary company of Permanent Gunners in 1812, after Lienhart and Humbert.

Second class artillery guard towards 1812-1814, after Job. The artillery guards wore a blue coat, scarlet turnbacks and facings, a blue collar decorated with one, two or three buttons depending on the class.

Permanent Gunner from an ordinary company during the Empire, wearing the Foot Artillery uniform.

THE PERMANENT COMPANIES AND THE NATIONAL GUARD

National Guard gunner in 1812, serving in the coastal batteries. The entirely blue coat was edged with scarlet on the collar, the lapels and the facings.

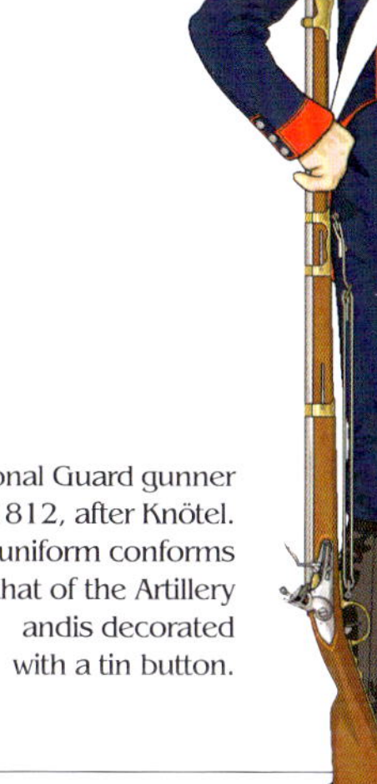

National Guard gunner in 1812, after Knötel. The uniform conforms to that of the Artillery andis decorated with a tin button.

National Guard gunner in service dress in 1812.

THE NATIONAL VETERANS

The drummers in the Veterans' Companies were children of the regiment aged 6 to 14 with a uniform with white braid.

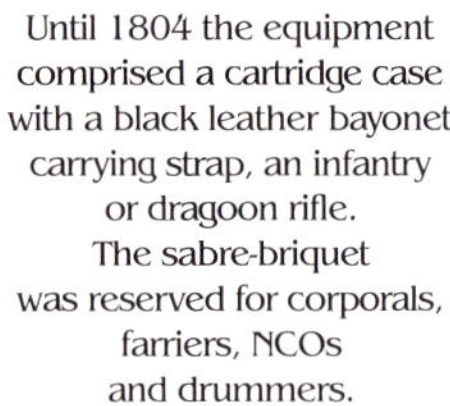

Until 1804 the equipment comprised a cartridge case with a black leather bayonet carrying strap, an infantry or dragoon rifle. The sabre-briquet was reserved for corporals, farriers, NCOs and drummers.

Sergeant-major standard-bearer wearing full dress according to Rigo. The NCOs in the Veterans did not wear epaulets.

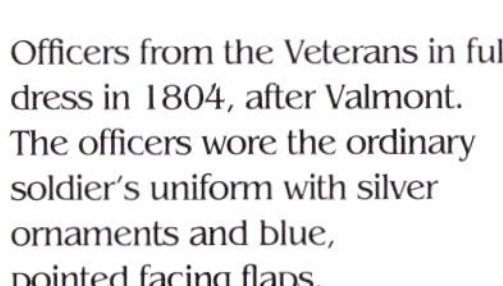

Officers from the Veterans in full dress in 1804, after Valmont. The officers wore the ordinary soldier's uniform with silver ornaments and blue, pointed facing flaps.

From 5 December 1804 onwards, each battalion received an eagle and a Picot-type flag with the inscription L'EMPEREUR/ DES FRANCAIS/A LA ..ME DEMI-BRIGADE/ DE VETERANS on the obverse side, and LE COURAGE/NE VIEILLIT PAS/…ME BATAILLON on the reverse.

THE NATIONAL VETERANS

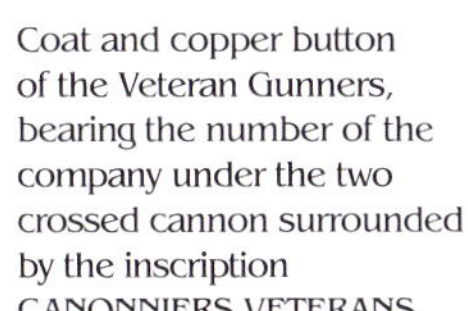

Coat and copper button of the Veteran Gunners, bearing the number of the company under the two crossed cannon surrounded by the inscription CANONNIERS VETERANS.

Veteran from a fusilier company wearing full summer dress in 1810, with white lining and no ornaments on the turnbacks.

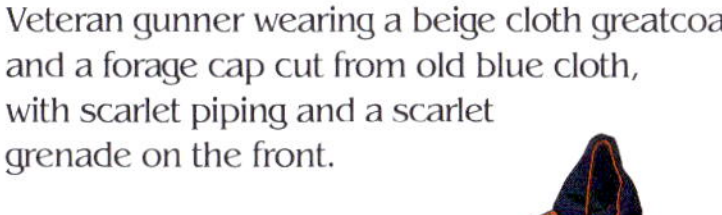

Veteran gunner wearing a beige cloth greatcoat and a forage cap cut from old blue cloth, with scarlet piping and a scarlet grenade on the front.

Veteran drummer in 1810, wearing the soldier's uniform without any stripes.

Veteran gunner in 1810 wearing the Foot Artillery uniform, according to the regulations.

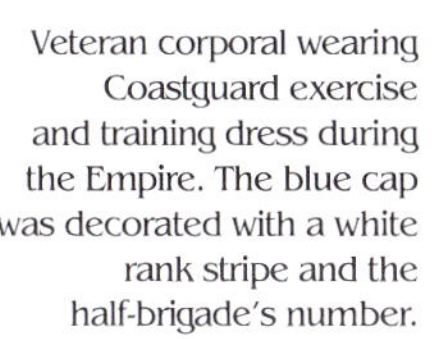

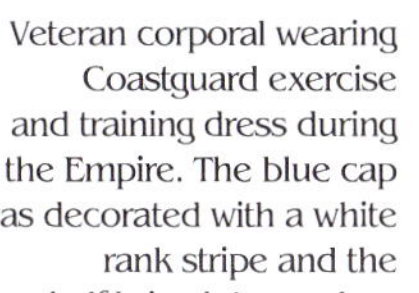

Veteran corporal wearing Coastguard exercise and training dress during the Empire. The blue cap was decorated with a white rank stripe and the half-brigade's number.

THE NATIONAL VETERANS

In 1812, each battalion received a vertically striped tricolour flag surmounted by a copper point. The obverse bore the inscription L'EMPEREUR/NAPOLEON/AU ...ME BATAILLON/DE VETERANS/NATIONAUX and the reverse wouldn't have borne the names of any battle.

Officer in a battalion of veterans according to the 1812 Regulations

Veteran gunner in full dress towards 1813-1815. The uniform was still that of the Foot Artillery, with blue collar, red facings and blue flaps.

Veteran fusilier wearing a grey greatcoat decorated with three seniority chevrons.

Veteran wearing full dress according to the 1812 Regulations. The skirts bear the letter N. The infantry shako replaced the old hat only from 1812 onwards.

THE TEAM TRAINS

Military transport button, stamped with a Phrygian cap during the Revolution.

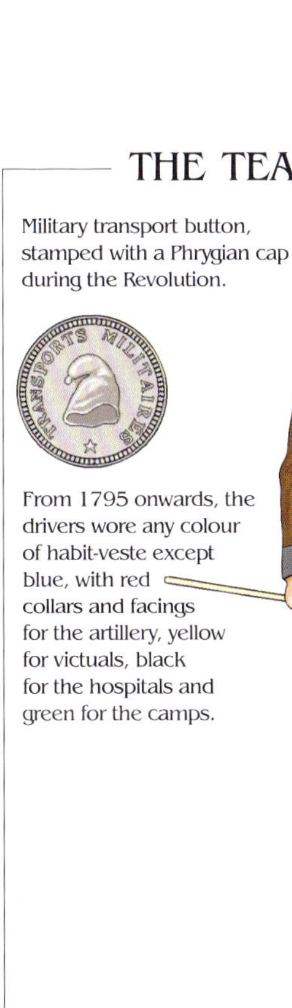

From 1795 onwards, the drivers wore any colour of habit-veste except blue, with red collars and facings for the artillery, yellow for victuals, black for the hospitals and green for the camps.

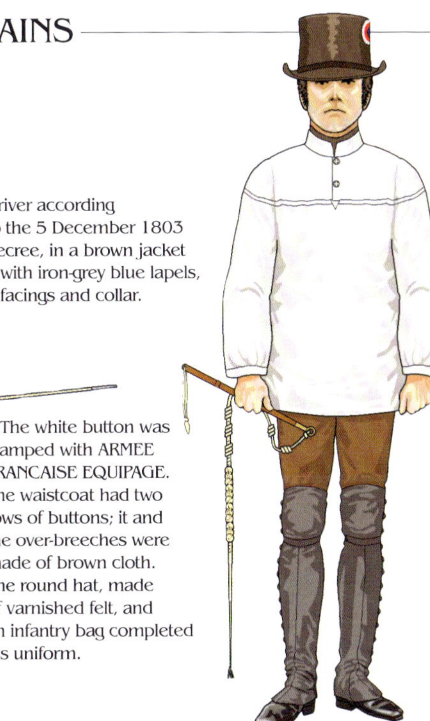

Driver according to the 5 December 1803 decree, in a brown jacket with iron-grey blue lapels, facings and collar.

The white button was stamped with ARMEE FRANCAISE EQUIPAGE. The waistcoat had two rows of buttons; it and the over-breeches were made of brown cloth. The round hat, made of varnished felt, and an infantry bag completed his uniform.

Driver wearing a jacket for stable work at the beginning of the Empire.

Driver wearing brown canvas trousers, after Rousselot.

Maréchal-des-logis Driver from 1806 onwards, according to Rousselot. The uniform became military with the habit-veste, the hat surmounted by a plume, the *écuyère*-style boots and the infantry sabre.

Driver wearing marching dress, 1806.

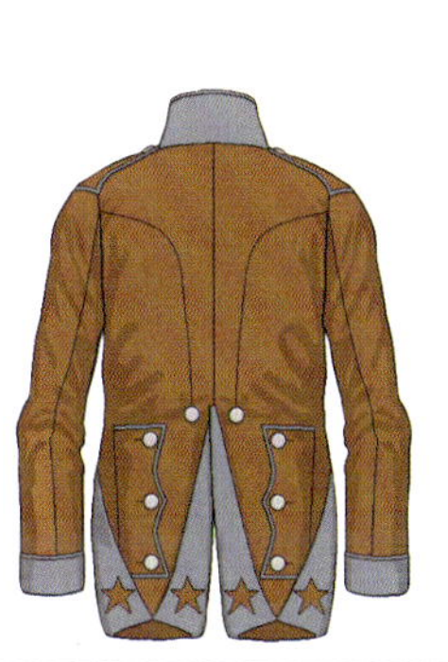

Driver dressed according to the plan to organise a First Battalion dated 25 December 1807.

to be too much of a burden on the state finances. It quickly became clear that the solution was to *"militarise the military teams"* which is what the Emperor decided to do on 26 March 1807 by organising the military transport teams into 8 four-company battalions.

Each of these companies comprised two divisions which themselves were organised into two squads. Each company had 34 caissons, a trail rope, a campaign forge, seven saddle horses, 144 draught horses and eight haut-de-pied horses (unharnessed horses).

The following year, on 4 May 1808, instructions fixed once and for all *"the organisation, the management, the administration and the accounts of the depots for the Military Team Trains established at Commercy"*.

Between 1807 and 1812, the Team Trains increased from eight battalions to twenty and it wasn't before 1811 that the make up of the Team battalions was modified. After these new units were created, the organisation had to be redefined.

The battalions of the Line deployed up to 252 wagons, each weighing 1,433 lbs and carrying 2,645 lbs of supplies.

- The *à la comtoise* battalions each used 606 wagons.
- The ox-drawn battalions used 306 wagons
- A battalion of pack mule teams was created in 1811. It was called the 1st Light Military Team Battalion (*1er bataillon léger des équipages militaires*).

In February 1811 three battalions of the Military Team Trains – the 2nd, 9th and 12th – were increased to six companies instead of the four originally planned. In April 1811, new changes were made to the Team Trains and thus the Tenth Battalion was also increased to six companies. The first two used wagons; the other four used pack mules.

In 1812, the 14th and 15th Battalions were in theory equipped with four-wheel light *à la comtoise* wagons. Once again, these battalions had six companies. The 16th and 17th, then the 20th and 21st were organised in the same way whilst the 22nd and 23rd supplied the teams needed for the ox carts.

The 18th and 19th Battalions were so-called *"ambulances"*. The 19th never formed up. The 24th was

(continued on page 78)

BEFORE THE TEAM TRAINS

Before the Team Trains were finally militarised in 1807, transport in the Grand Armée was the responsibility of the Breidt Company. This company owned the horses and replaced them at its own expense. The caissons and the harnesses belonged to the State. The company rented the caissons to the State and was not to use them for anything not stipulated in the contract. The brigade personnel were recruited by the company and were therefore not soldiers like the others.

Breidt provided headquarters with a general agent, a section head, three clerks, 75 drivers and 200 *haut de pied* horses.

A team inspection service under the responsibility of an inspector-general was set up by the central administration; it sent its inspectors to all the army corps headquarters. The military teams had *"at all times* (war and peace) *to take charge of camp and clothing items, the mobile hospitals, supplies, and for the army, the auxiliary pool service"*.

The contract signed with Breidt on 24 Floréal An XIII (14 May 1805) organised the team brigades that were to be assigned to the armies. The first six brigades (N° 1 to 6) – present in the *Camps de l'Océan* (the Ocean Camps) – used 163 wagons and 640 horses in all. 24 brigades were formed at Sampigny and Paris and joined the Grande Armée. The 26 brigades in the *Grande Armée* (2,610 horses) – the others had joined the Army of the North – supplied the teams for 546 wagons.

The organisation of these brigades was not suited to wartime. The four horse caissons were driven by a single man without a replacement if he was killed, wounded or ill. The civilian wagoners only travelled three or four leagues per day, and the horses, being the property of the company, were cosseted without any regard for tactical and strategic requirements.

Breidt employed 1,067 men in the teams at the end of 1806. They were organised into sections each having a head assisted by divisional heads, and the drivers, the latter being organised into regular brigades. This organisation was drawn up on 14 September 1805: one civilian employee, with the title of captain commanded the brigade; his assistants had military sounding names like adjudant, *maréchal des logis-chef*, furrier, two brigadiers. The brigade comprised three workers and 30 soldiers – the drivers.

At the beginning of 1807, the Emperor decided to get rid of Breidt which was having trouble supplying 700 caissons let alone supply the 3,000 that were needed; he decided to reorganise the military team service and to make them a proper subdivision of the Grande Armée.

THE TEAM TRAINS

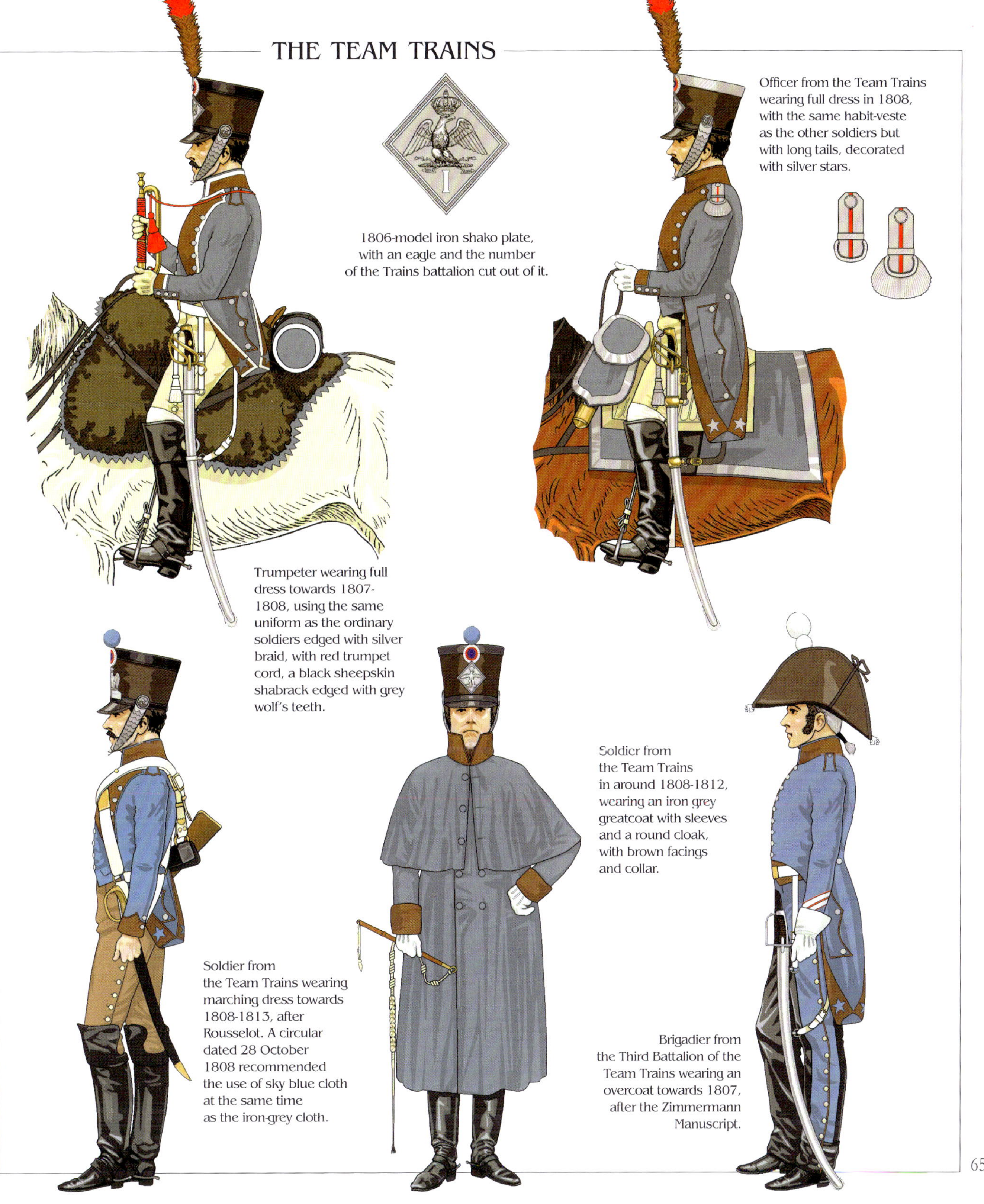

1806-model iron shako plate, with an eagle and the number of the Trains battalion cut out of it.

Officer from the Team Trains wearing full dress in 1808, with the same habit-veste as the other soldiers but with long tails, decorated with silver stars.

Trumpeter wearing full dress towards 1807-1808, using the same uniform as the ordinary soldiers edged with silver braid, with red trumpet cord, a black sheepskin shabrack edged with grey wolf's teeth.

Soldier from the Team Trains in around 1808-1812, wearing an iron grey greatcoat with sleeves and a round cloak, with brown facings and collar.

Soldier from the Team Trains wearing marching dress towards 1808-1813, after Rousselot. A circular dated 28 October 1808 recommended the use of sky blue cloth at the same time as the iron-grey cloth.

Brigadier from the Third Battalion of the Team Trains wearing an overcoat towards 1807, after the Zimmermann Manuscript.

THE TEAM TRAINS

Flat uniform button for the Team Trains made of tinplate, stamped with the battalion number.

Brigadier-farrier from the Team Trains, armed with a carbine or a musketoon, and a light cavalry sabre like all the NCOs and non-driving soldiers.

Team Train driver towards 1807-1808. The coat with short tails was cut from iron-grey cloth; it had pointed lapels, with a brown collar, facings and lining. The clasped turnbacks were decorated with grey stars. The plate-less shako was decorated with a brown, red-tipped plume.

Trumpeter from the Team Trains in 1808 wearing a uniform with inversed colours according to the Hamburg Burgher's Manuscript.

Plate with an eagle cut out made of tin the base has the battalion number cut out of it.

Soldier from the Team Trains wearing an overcoat towards 1808, after the Hamburg Burgher. The hat had a strange pompom and the turnbacks were decorated with white stars.

Soldier from the Team Trains wearing campaign dress in 1808 after the Hamburg Manuscript. Note the waistcoat entirely edged with brown.

THE TEAM TRAINS

Soldier from the Team Trains in the 5th Corps of the Reserve Army in 1811, after the Hamburg Manuscript.

Team Trains soldier wearing stable dress with a knitted jacket and canvas trousers, according to the Hamburg Burgher, in 1808.

Blacksmith from the Team Trains in the Fifth Army Corps, according to Hamburg Burgher in 1808.

Team Train driver wearing full dress towards 1808-1813, after Rousselot. Like all the drivers, he carried the sabre-briquet and baldric in use in the artillery train.

Worker in the provisional company of the Team Trains, created on 1 December 1809 in Spain, after Rousselot. This dress was distinguished with dark blue of the elite company of workers, and was confirmed by an organisational decree on 1 January 1811.

Officer in the Team Trains of the 5th Corps in the Army Reserve in 1811, according to the Hamburg Manuscript.

Chevillier (front horse) of a French-style harnessing, after Rousselot.

Team Train driver wearing full dress in 1808-1813, after Rousselot. The white waistcoat was usually used for full dress.

Light carriage or ambulance driver, wearing road dress in 1812-1813, after Rousselot.

Thill-horse (the *Limonier* - the first horse placed between the shafts) of a French style harnessing, after Rousselot.

THE TEAM TRAINS

Trumpeter from the First Battalion of the Team Trains in 1812, after Job (as far as Valmont was concerned, he was more likely the driver of an artillery train).

Soldier from the Team Trains wearing an iron-grey cloth cloak with a hood in around 1812-1814, after Rousselot.

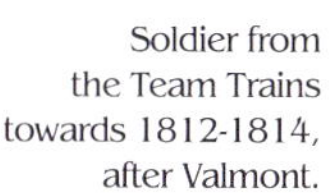

Soldier from the Team Trains towards 1812-1814, after Valmont.

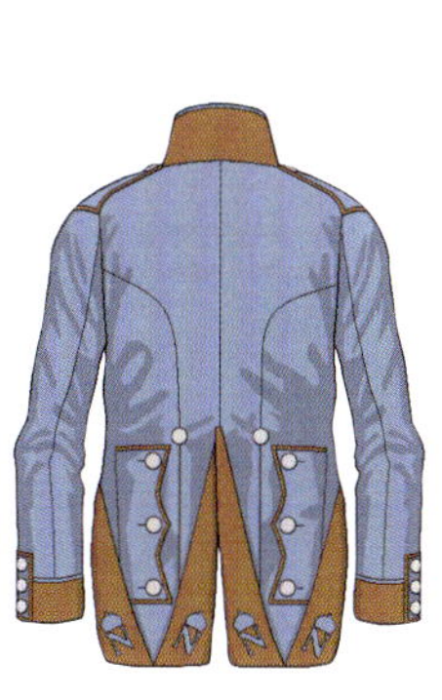

Worker from the Team Trains wearing trousers towards 1812-1814, after Valmont.

Soldier in the Team Trains, from the company of pool workers, towards 1812-1812, after Boisselier.

Team Train driver wearing campaign dress in about 1813-1814.

THE TEAM TRAINS

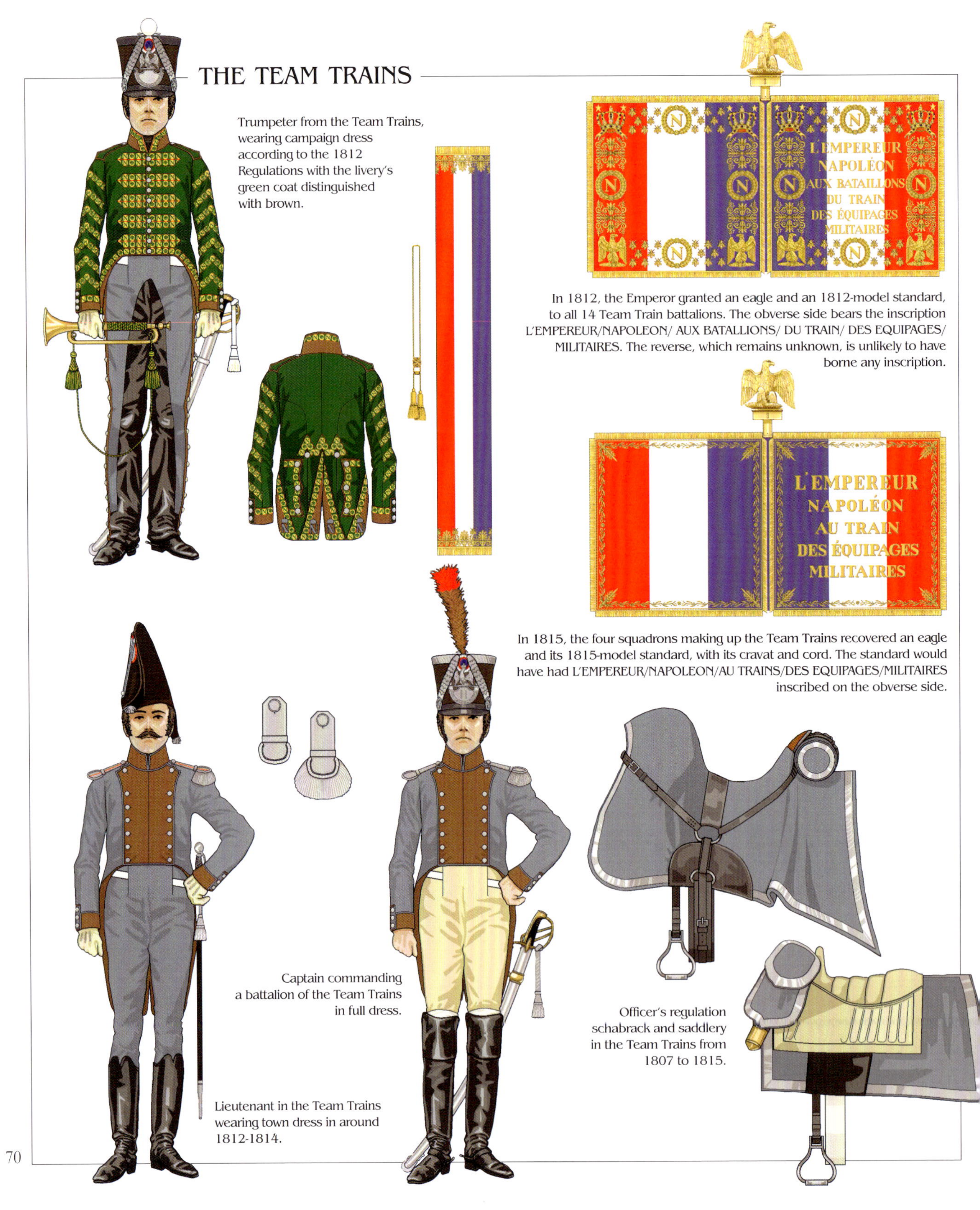

Trumpeter from the Team Trains, wearing campaign dress according to the 1812 Regulations with the livery's green coat distinguished with brown.

In 1812, the Emperor granted an eagle and an 1812-model standard, to all 14 Team Train battalions. The obverse side bears the inscription L'EMPEREUR/NAPOLEON/ AUX BATALLIONS/ DU TRAIN/ DES EQUIPAGES/ MILITAIRES. The reverse, which remains unknown, is unlikely to have borne any inscription.

In 1815, the four squadrons making up the Team Trains recovered an eagle and its 1815-model standard, with its cravat and cord. The standard would have had L'EMPEREUR/NAPOLEON/AU TRAINS/DES EQUIPAGES/MILITAIRES inscribed on the obverse side.

Captain commanding a battalion of the Team Trains in full dress.

Officer's regulation schabrack and saddlery in the Team Trains from 1807 to 1815.

Lieutenant in the Team Trains wearing town dress in around 1812-1814.

THE TEAM TRAINS

Soldier from the Team Trains wearing an iron-grey stable jacket, with a forage cap edged with brown, according to the 1812 Regulations.

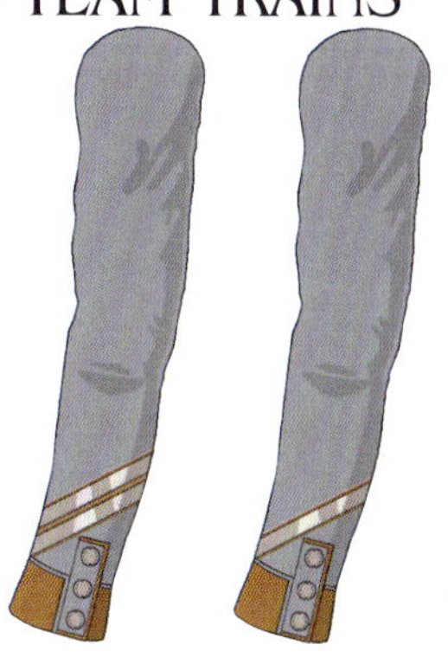

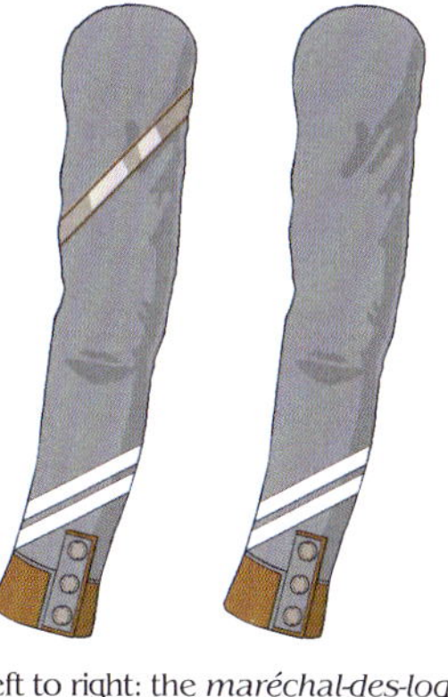

Team Train NCOs' rank distinctions for, from left to right: the *maréchal-des-logis* chef, the *maréchal-des-logis*, the brigadier farrier and the brigadier.

Soldier in the Team Trains wearing a sleeveless waistcoat, according to the 1812 Regulations.

1812-model shako plate made of tinplate, with lion's heads and the battalion number cut out of the escutcheon.

Team Train driver wearing full dress made of 1812 iron-grey cloth with turnbacks decorated with crowned Ns.

Team Train driver according to the regulations put into practice during the First Restoration. This iron grey worn no doubt in some companies was entirely edged with chamois.

Maréchal des Logis from a light Team Train company in Spain, after Vanson. The uniform corresponds to the 1814 Regulations, with chamois coloured edging, epaulets and pompom.

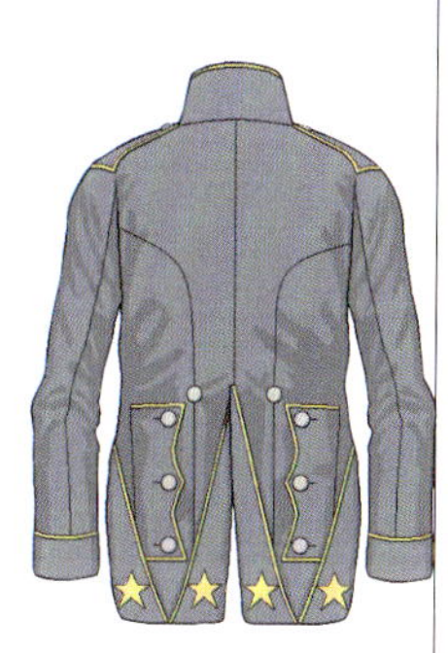

THE GRIBEAUVAL TRIQUEBALLE

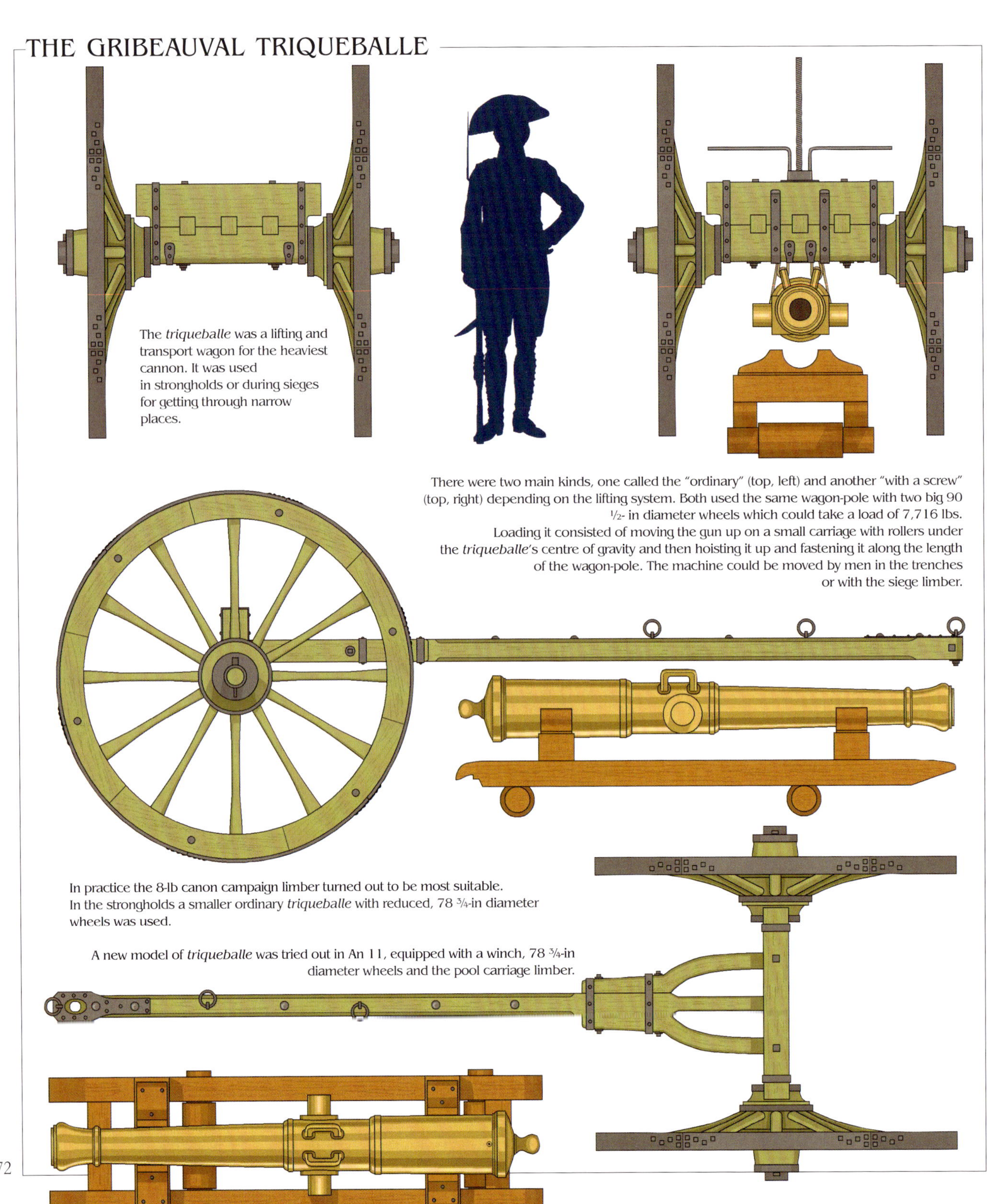

The *triqueballe* was a lifting and transport wagon for the heaviest cannon. It was used in strongholds or during sieges for getting through narrow places.

There were two main kinds, one called the "ordinary" (top, left) and another "with a screw" (top, right) depending on the lifting system. Both used the same wagon-pole with two big 90 ½- in diameter wheels which could take a load of 7,716 lbs.
Loading it consisted of moving the gun up on a small carriage with rollers under the *triqueballe*'s centre of gravity and then hoisting it up and fastening it along the length of the wagon-pole. The machine could be moved by men in the trenches or with the siege limber.

In practice the 8-lb canon campaign limber turned out to be most suitable.
In the strongholds a smaller ordinary *triqueballe* with reduced, 78 ¾-in diameter wheels was used.

A new model of *triqueballe* was tried out in An 11, equipped with a winch, 78 ¾-in diameter wheels and the pool carriage limber.

THE GRIBEAUVAL TRANSPORT CART

Heavy 16- and 24-lb siege guns, or howitzer and mortar barrels were moved using a load-carrying cart so as to preserve the gun carriages. Also called the canon cart, this carriage comprised two axles, adjustable to the size of the load.

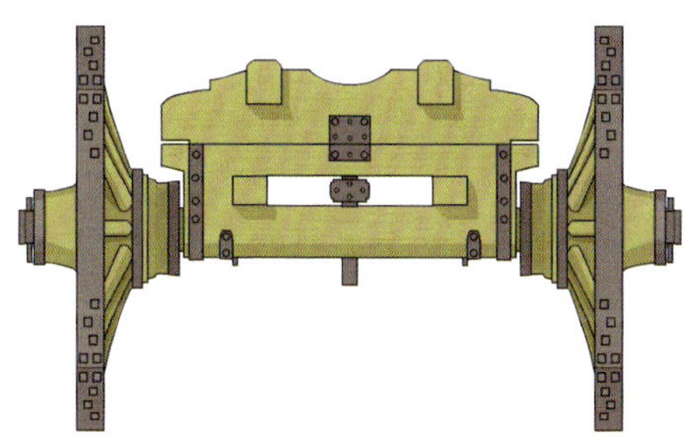

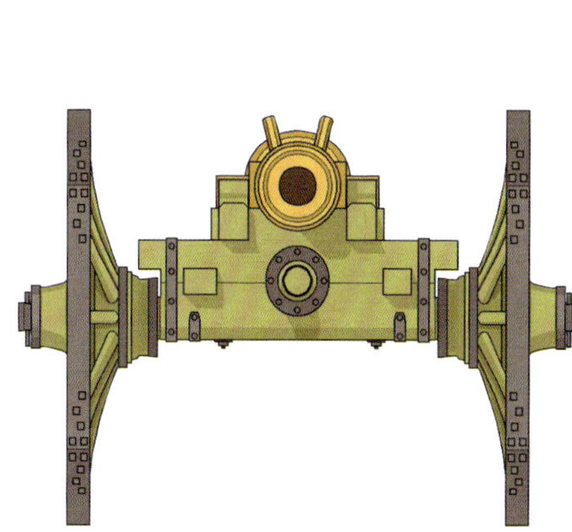

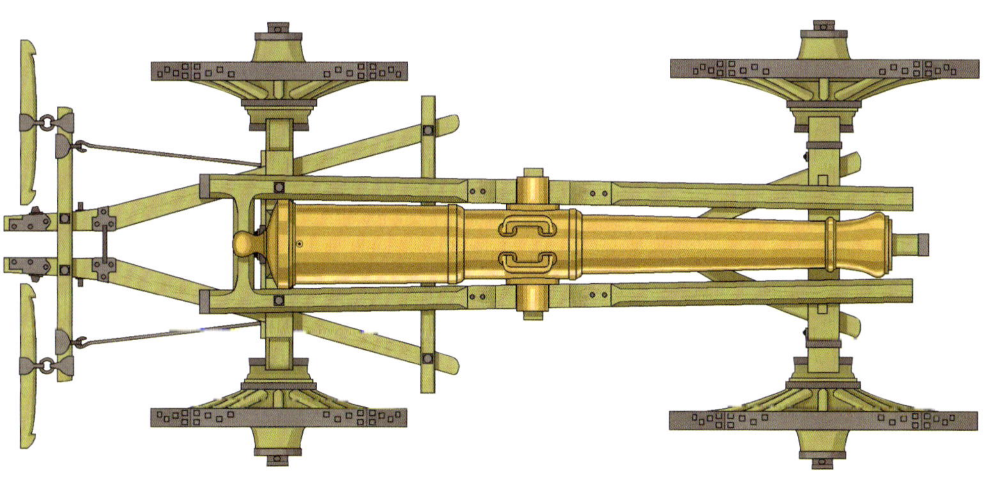

The barrel was firmly wedged on a wooden litter fitted with recesses for the trunnions, with two braces to support the barrel and the breech. This chariot, also used in the arsenals and the foundries, had two large 58 ¼-in diameter wheels on the rear Train axle and 49 ½-in wheels on the front axle.

THE GRIBEAUVAL MORTAR TRUCK

The shaft truck, also called the mortar truck, was used for transporting a siege mortar. This very simply designed carriage comprised a platform on two wheels, with shafts and no sides. Four horses were needed to draw a truck carrying a 10-in mortar, loaded by means of a hoisting crane.

THE SHORT GRIBEAUVAL AMMUNITION CART

A special wagon was used for moving up a large number of projectiles during a siege. It was the same as the shaft truck but it had sides. The cannonballs, shells and other bombs were loaded loose on the plateau and unloaded by merely tipping it up near the batteries. As only two horses were needed to draw the cart, it was able to move around in very cramped spaces.

THE LONG GRIBEAUVAL AMMUNITION CART

This was exactly the same as the short cart except for its length; it was used only for transporting ammunition during a siege. All the carts were built according to the same model with 58 ¼-in diameter wheels.

THE GRIBEAUVAL SIEGE FRONT LIMBER

The siege limber (front axle) was common to all siege and stronghold guns, with a 36.6- in diameter wheel, a total length of 9 ft 1 ½ in and a weight of 617 $^1/_3$ lbs.

THE TEAM TRAINS IN RUSSIA

During the Russian Campaign, on the road to Vitebsk, the rear did not follow quickly enough. The Emperor ordered the convoys to hurry up: according to him they had to cover *"at least six leagues a day"*. He also had it known that *"any officer in the military teams who took more than ten days to go from Vilna to Glubokoya... would be finished and noted as bein a laggard on the road and doing his duties badly."*

(in Dictionnaire de la Grande Armée, Alain Pigeard)

made up of Poles and was assigned to the Grand Duchy of Warsaw.

On 23 February 1813, General Baron Joseph Denis Picard was appointed Inspector General of the Teams.

In the presence of the enemy or even when the headquarters thought there might be some "business", the teams remained at the rear.

The troops were in fact constantly deprived of the teams, often for several days and officers had to take the necessary measures.

THE REGIMENTAL ARTILLERY

In 1793, the revolutionaries in charge of running the War gave each infantry half-brigade a company of volunteer gunners to serve six 4-lb guns. This system disappeared with the half-brigades.

In 1809 after the terrible battles of Aspern and Essling, Regimental Artillery reappeared briefly. On 24 May 1809 an order form the Emperor gave two 3-pounders and their caissons to each of the regiments in Davout's corps.

A decree dated June 1809 stipulated that *" two 3- or 4-pounders, three caissons, a campaign forge, and ambulance caisson and a caisson for transporting the regimental papers would be attached to each infantry regiment of the Line and of the Light Infantry. These wagons will always advance with the battalion where the regimental Eagle is held."*

Unfortunately not all the Army of Germany infantry regiments were concerned by the decree (see opposite). On 11 April 1810 a new decree suppressed the materiel of the companies attached to each infantry regiment; the guns, caissons, forges and horses were withdrawn upon their return to France or Italy.

For the Russian Campaign, the 11 February 1811 decree stipulated that the Regimental Artillery would comprise four cannon, 18 caissons, a forge, 60 gunners (officers included), 60 soldiers of the Train, and 100 horses for the regiments which were part of the *Corps d'observation de l'Elbe* (the Elba Observation Corps), the future 1st and 2nd Corps (12th, 17th, 21st, 25th, 30th, 43rd, 48th, 57th, 61st, 85th, 108th, 111th Line Infantry Regiments and the 2nd, 7th, 13th, and 33rd Light Infantry Regiments). There were however never enough guns to satisfy the orders.

The Russian Campaign marked the end of this attempt to give the Infantry a "close" support artillery.

THE REGIMENTS EQUIPPED WITH ARTILLERY PIECES IN 1809

2e de ligne	42e de ligne	108e de ligne
3e de ligne	46e de ligne	111e de ligne,
4e de ligne	48e de ligne	112e de ligne
5e de ligne	52e de ligne	3e léger
8e de ligne	53e de ligne	6e léger
9e de ligne	56e de ligne	7e léger
11e de ligne	57e de ligne	8e léger
12e de ligne	60e de ligne	9e léger,
13e de ligne	61e de ligne	10e léger
17e de ligne	62e de ligne	13e léger
18e de ligne	65e de ligne	14e léger,
19e de ligne	79e de ligne	15e léger
21e de ligne	81e de ligne	18e léger
23e de ligne	84e de ligne	22e léger
24e de ligne	85e de ligne	23e léger
25e de ligne	92e de ligne	24e léger
27e de ligne	93e de ligne	+ the 4th Battalion
29e de ligne	94e de ligne	of the 39th, 40th
30e de ligne	95e de ligne	and 88th of the
33e de ligne	102e de ligne	Line
35e de ligne	105e de ligne	
37e de ligne	106e de ligne	

REGIMENTAL ARTILLERY

Gunner in the Infantry of the Line in around 1811, wearing the Grenadier uniform modified to the colours of the Artillery.

Sergeant in the Regimental Artillery of the Line wearing full dress towards 1811-1813, after Bénigni.

Light Infantry gunner wearing marching dress towards 1811-1813, after Bénigni. Each company had two 3- and 5-lb Austrian cannon.

Driver from the 2nd Infantry Regiment of the Line artillery wearing marching dress, after Bénigni. At that date the drivers did not yet have a shortcoat or any skin breeches, and rarely any boots.

THE REGIMENTAL ARTILLERY

Gunner in the Light Infantry wearing campaign dress in around 1811-1813, according to Bénigni. As an elite unit, the gunners wore the uniform of their respective regiments, which was modified by items similar to those of the Foot Artillery and the Artillery Train.

Sous-lieutenant commanding the regimental artillery train in the Light Infantry, towards 1811-1815, after Bucquoy.

Driver in the Light Infantry, wearing campaign dress towards 1811-1813, according to Bénigni.

Driver in the regimental artillery of the Line wearing full dress in 1812, after Bégnini. The portmanteau was not included in the bundle.

Sergeant-major in the regimental artillery in the Light Infantry in 1811 after Knötel.

Lieutenant commanding a regimental artillery company of the Line, wearing marching dress in around 1811-1813.

Regimental artillery driver in the Light Infantry, wearing marching dress in about 1812, after Bénigni.

Officer commanding the artillery company of the 6th Infantry Regiment of the Line in 1812, according to Rigo.

Gunner in the 6th Infantry Regiment of the Line in 1812, after Rigo.

Gunner in the regimental artillery of the Line according to the 1812 Regulations.

Sources and short bibliography

— Volumes I and IV of "Règlement sur l'habit" from Bardin.

— *Le Plumet*. Plates nos 13, 76, 113,114, 164,169. Rigo. *Chez l'auteur*.

— L'Armée française. Plates from L. Rousselot Dedicated to the artillery of the line and the artillery of the Guard.

— L'uniforme et les armes des soldats du 1er Empire, L. et F. Funcken. *Casterman*.

— Équipement militaire de 1600 à 1870. Michel Pétard. *Chez l'auteur*.

— L'Artillerie Gribeauval. R. Ducoin. *Hors-série from CFFH*.

— L'Artillerie, de l'Ancien Régime à 1830. *Hors-série from carnets de la Sabretache*.

— Les uniformes de l'armée française. Dr Lienhart et R. Humbert. *Librairie Buhl*.

— Guide à l'usage des artistes et costumiers. H. Malibran.

— Plates from Martinet. Bertrand Malvaux. *Éditions du Canonnier*.

— Officers and soldiers. The Imperial Guard, volume I. André Jouineau, J.-M. Mongin. *Histoire & Collections*.

— Officers and soldiers. The Imperial Guard, volume V. André Jouineau. *Histoire & Collections*.

— Le canonnier à cheval. Michel Pétard. *Uniformes* n° 43

— Le canonnier à pied de la Garde. Michel Pétard in *Uniformes* n° 69.

— L'artillerie du Premier Empire. *Tradition magazine*, special issue n° 78-79.

— Le Dictionnaire de la Grande Armée, Alain Pigeard. *Éditions Tallandier*

— Napoleon Specialist Troops, Philipp Haythornthwaite, *Men at Arms #199, Osprey*

Design and Layout by Ludovic Letrun — Book executed by the Studio *"Éditions des Soixante"*, supervised by Jean-Marie Mongin for *Histoire & Collections*

ISBN: 978-2-35250-432-0
Publisher's number: 35250

A BOOK PUBLISHED BY
HISTOIRE & COLLECTIONS
5, AVENUE DE LA RÉPUBLIQUE
75011 PARIS - FRANCE
Tel: +33 (0) 1 40 21 18 20
Fax: +33 (0) 1 47 00 51 11
www.histoireetcollections.com

Print by Calidad Grafica
in Spain, European Union,
in March 2016.